ALEXANDRE DUMAS'

Adventures in Algeria

The *Véloce*

ALEXANDRE DUMAS'

Adventures in Algeria

Translated by

ALMA ELIZABETH MURCH

CHILTON COMPANY—BOOK DIVISION
Publishers
Philadelphia   *New York*

LIBRARY OF CONGRESS CATALOG CARD NUMBER 59-13112

MANUFACTURED IN THE UNITED STATES OF AMERICA
BY QUINN & BODEN COMPANY, INC., RAHWAY, N. J.

Foreword

❦ ❦ ❦

In November, 1846, Alexandre Dumas was in Cadiz with a few close friends who had accompanied him on his tour of Spain, described in *Adventures in Spain*, published by Chilton Company in 1959. Before leaving Paris, Dumas had been asked by M. de Salvandy, *le ministre de l'instruction publique*, to visit Algeria and write a description of his travels in that country. Just at this period, France was very anxious to encourage emigration to her recently acquired territories on the other side of the Mediterranean, partly to stabilize conditions in Algeria and develop the natural resources of this new colony, partly to relieve unemployment and other economic difficulties at home. Doubtless, the Minister felt that Dumas, with his power of making everything he described seem exciting and attractive and his popularity with all classes of the reading public, could do a great deal to stimulate an interest in the country, and so further the government's plan.

For many years Dumas had longed to visit Algeria—he was actually packing to go there in July, 1830, but was prevented from leaving Paris by the outbreak of the Revolution known as *"Les Trois Glorieuses"*—and he enthusiastically accepted M. de Salvandy's proposal, with the proviso that a French warship should be provided to take him across the Straits of Gibraltar on this "government mission." Whether or not M. de Salvandy was in order in agreeing to Dumas' stipulation

v

was hotly debated later in the *Tribune,* but the corvette *Le Véloce* duly appeared in Cadiz harbor and welcomed Dumas and his friends aboard for their voyage to Algeria.

They reached Algiers to find that the Governor, Marshal Bugeaud, not knowing precisely when Dumas would arrive, was away accompanying a group of visiting *députés* to a remote part of the country on a tour of inspection. Feeling disinclined to wait idly in Algiers for two or three weeks until the Governor's return, Dumas decided he would devote that time to seeing other places of interest farther to the east along the North African coast. Naturally, he assumed, the *Véloce,* having been "placed at his disposal," would take him wherever he chose to go! It says much for Dumas' prestige as a popular celebrity, his forceful exuberance, that he managed to override the astonished protests of naval authorities in Algiers and carry out his plan. So off he sailed, using a ship of the line as though it were his private yacht, directing her to put in wherever his fancy took him, even into Tunis, where a French warship had no right to be, and announcing his arrival there with a salute of twenty-one guns! Fortunately for international relations between France and the Regency of Tunis, then an independent state, the Bey received him cordially, and Dumas saw and heard much to interest him in Tunisia before sailing back along the coast to complete his tour of Algeria by the end of the year.

Dumas was uneasily aware that trouble was waiting for him in France, and once he was back in Paris the storm broke over his head with even greater violence than he had anticipated. January and February were taken up with lawsuits brought against him by furious editors of periodicals, chief among them being *La Presse, Commerce,* and the *Constitutionnel,* complaining that in the previous November Dumas had slipped off to Spain and Algeria without a word to his publishers, leaving them with *Joseph Balsamo, Le Batard de Mauléon* and other serials broken off in mid-air; stories, novels, articles promised by a given date, some of them even paid for in advance, and never produced. It was all only too true, and

Dumas was ordered to pay heavy costs and make good his "defalcations" within a specified time.

Besides grappling with this accumulation of literary work, Dumas spent hours every day in supervising the completion of his fantastic château near Port-Marly, which his friends named "Monte-Cristo." He was also frenziedly producing, in collaboration with Auguste Maquet, a dramatized version of his novel *La Reine Margot*, to be performed at the opening of his new Théâtre Historique in Paris on February 20, 1847.

While all this activity was at its height, the Chamber of Deputies debated *l'affaire du Véloce* in one of the stormiest sessions of the year. The *Ministre de la Marine* hotly challenged the action taken by the *Ministre de l'instruction publique*. What right had M. de Salvandy to order the movements of a French warship? It was absurd to call this visit to Algeria an "official mission." It was nothing of the sort! A complete misunderstanding! Throughout the debate, Dumas was contemptuously referred to as *"ce monsieur,"* or "this fabricator of romances"; M. Castellane made caustic comments, and M. Léon de Maleville went so far as to observe that the whole affair was a disgrace to the French flag!

Dumas was furious. His passport, issued especially for the occasion, stated clearly that he was *"chargé d'une mission du ministre de l'instruction publique";* he had received an official letter of welcome from the *gouvernement-général* of Algeria; he held ample proofs that he had been sent on a government mission; and the deputies had slandered him! He challenged M. Castellane to a duel, but that member of the Chamber retired behind the "inviolability of the *Tribune*" and made no reply. Dumas' correspondence on the same subject with M. de Maleville somehow found its way into the French press and was even quoted in the *Times:* [1]

Sir,

You insulted me the other day in the Chamber of Deputies. Free today from all business engagements, I send to you my friend,

1. Wednesday, March 3, 1847, p. 6, Col. 4. "M. Dumas once more."

M. Viennet, Peer of France, President of the Society of Men of Letters, to learn the day, the place and the hour—[we give the conclusion in the original French, lest it might be supposed we exaggerated] *où il vous convient que nous vous couperons la gorge.*

Alexandre Dumas, Marquis de la Pailleterie.[2]

To this strange epistle the sensible M. de Maleville sent the following amusing answer:

Sir,

I thank you for having afforded me the opportunity of seeing the agreeable and excellent M. Viennet. As to the proposal which you are good enough to make to cut my throat, I am chagrined beyond measure at not being able to accept it. I have not the honor to be your equal as a gentleman.

Le Marquis de Maleville.

With so many demands on his attention, it is not surprising that Dumas did not finish writing up his notes of his tour in North Africa until later in the year. The work was published in four volumes between 1848 and 1851. He had presented his travels through Spain in the form of letters to a mysterious "Madame," but, though he still occasionally addresses a comment to the same lady, this book is arranged as a continuous commentary on the places and people he saw in the course of his tour of North Africa, enriched with all the information about local affairs that would interest contemporary French readers.

In preparing this, the first[3] English translation of Dumas' travels in Algeria and Tunisia, and condensing it to about a quarter of the original length, it has been necessary to omit

2. The title Dumas used here was derived from his grandfather, Antoine Alexandre Davy, Marquis de la Pailleterie. His natural son, Thomas Alexandre, born in San Domingo of a Negress, Marie Cessette Dumas, became a French general and the father of Alexandre Dumas, who sometimes used the name of Davy as a pseudonym, and the title when it suited him to do so.

3. Some individual stories from Dumas' text were published in America in 1868 with the title *Tales of Algeria* (Philadelphia, Claxton, Ramsen and Heppelfinger); another extract, "The Sheikh," appeared in New York in *The Golden Book Magazine*, November, 1932.

matter that can be found elsewhere, particularly Dumas' detailed survey of the French conquest of Algeria, his versions of classical myths and legends relative to Africa, and certain material that Dumas himself used again in his *Causeries*. The result brings his actual journey into stronger relief and gives a vivid picture of the palaces and private homes he visited, the military camps and Arab tents, the markets, brothels, inns, shrines and Roman settlements, the deep-rooted antipathies of race and blood which cause the same problems today as they did a hundred years and more ago. Dumas' account brings to life one of the most exciting, eventful journeys made by this indomitable and indefatigable traveler.

A. E. MURCH

Contents

❧   ❧   ❧

1

⚜ ⚜ ⚜

DEPARTURE FROM CADIZ

As you will remember from my earlier letters, Madame, when the Minister of Public Education saw me in Paris and invited me to visit Algeria after touring Spain, he assured me that on a certain date a French warship would be waiting at Cadiz to convey me and my friends across the Straits to Africa. When, however, I wrote from Seville to M. Huet, our French consul at Cadiz, inquiring whether the promised vessel had arrived, he replied that no naval ship of any nation had put in at Cadiz for more than a week. This was disquieting news, for we had already stayed three days longer than I had anticipated in Seville, partly because of the festivities so hospitably arranged there in my honor, partly in the hope of hearing from my son, Alexandre, who had unaccountably disappeared. So it was in a state of some anxiety that we sailed down the Guadalquivir and arrived at Cadiz on Wednesday, November 18, 1846.

Eagerly we scanned the forest of masts in the harbor, and were overjoyed when we managed to make out the funnels of not merely one, but two steamships, each flying the tricolor. The moment our boat touched the quay I jumped ashore, and, leaving my companions to see to our luggage, ran to inquire at the Customs House. I learned that there were, indeed, two French warships lying at anchor: the *Achéron*, which, after three days in port, was on the point of sailing on a good-will mission to Morocco, with M. Duchâteau, the French consul at Tangier, bearing gifts to Abd-el-Rhaman from the King of France; and the *Véloce*, which had arrived the evening before and would shortly be leaving for an unknown destination. At once, all my hopes were centered on the *Véloce*.

We passed through Customs with the usual difficulties and were barely settled in our hotel, the Europa, when the *mozo* announced a visitor, M. Vial, second officer of the corvette *Véloce*. Despite all the anxieties of the past few days and my friends' doubts as to whether the Minister's promise could be relied on, I had been at some pains to preserve the serenity proper to the leader of an expedition and to admit no uncertainty. Now I just had time for a triumphant glance at my companions, who bowed to acknowledge that I had been right, before M. Vial was shown in. He had been sent by Captain Bérard, the officer commanding the *Véloce*, to greet me and present an official dispatch from the Governor-General of Algeria, welcoming me to that country and placing the *Véloce* at my service for the duration of my visit.[1] I thanked M. Vial for his trouble, and as dinner was announced at that moment I invited him to join our table.

During dinner, questions and answers flew back and forth. Was the *Véloce* a fast ship? Was her captain friendly and approachable? Would the weather be good? We gathered that the *Véloce* was rather slow, being too heavy for her engines, and even on her good days she made no more than about seven or eight knots, but that she was a fine craft, steady even in rough seas. As for Captain Bérard, he was a man of 40 or 45 years, punctiliously correct in manner (as most naval officers are), grave and taciturn, with a reputation of never having laughed while on duty. With all our French gaiety, it was most unlikely that we should succeed in making him smile. The weather? It would certainly be fine, and Maquet, who had almost died of seasickness on our

1. In the original text, Dumas reproduced his official invitation in full, to refute the statement made by the *Ministre de Marine*, who insisted that the whole affair was due to a misunderstanding.—*Ed.*

trip down the Guadalquivir, began to take fresh heart for the voyage. Dinner was a hilarious meal, and M. Vial had ample opportunity of seeing how high spirited we could be, while we found him to be a thoroughly congenial guest, parting from him on excellent terms.

It was agreed that at noon on the morrow we would go aboard the *Véloce* to pay our respects to the Captain, but at eleven, while we were still busily preparing for the visit, Captain Bérard paid us a ceremonious call himself. We were somewhat discomfited by his scrupulous courtesy, but before he left us, four hours later, I think he was as delighted to have us as passengers as we were to have him as captain, and he invited us to inspect his ship on the following day.

Punctually at the time agreed we drew alongside the *Véloce*. The Captain awaited us at the head of the gangway, with the whole ship's company drawn up on deck as the bosun piped us aboard, and after welcoming us he led us straight down to the wardroom, being convinced that we could not have had a square meal since leaving Bayonne. It was a spacious apartment, still bearing traces of the honors paid to earlier passengers[2] in its gilded moldings and the crimson silk curtains screening the doors of five cabins leading off it. Three of these cabins were allotted to Boulanger, myself, and Alexandre (in the hope that he would rejoin us before we sailed); the fourth was the Captain's own, while the fifth and largest, right in the bow, was offered to Maquet and Giraud. They, however, after having a word with M. Vial, asked to be accommodated in the officers' quarters amidships, where the vessel's movement could hardly be felt. As for Desbarolles, he boasted loudly of being fully accustomed to Neptune's caprices but preferred not to commit himself as to where he would sleep. We were not unduly worried on that score, for there were still five empty cabins—more than enough for him and his carbine. Vial, too, kindly offered us the use of his own deck cabin. It was very small, just large

2. The *Véloce*, launched in 1838, had been used by King Louis Philippe when returning from his visit to England in 1844.

enough to take a table and a chair besides his bunk, but the continuous draft between the door and the window was a godsend in hot weather.

The gunnery officer was presented to us and I was delighted to meet him, for all our weapons were in need of skilled attention. We were asked to make a complete list of them and hand it to him personally when we came aboard.

So we returned to Cadiz, more than delighted with the ship, her captain, and the officers serving under him. If Giraud and Maquet were somewhat less enthusiastic than the rest of us at the prospect of sailing in her, you already know the reason. (I forgot to mention earlier that it was only by lying flat on deck, all the way from Sanlúcar to Cadiz, that Giraud managed to avoid sharing Maquet's indisposition on the Guadalquivir.) All next day and the day after, while my friends explored Cadiz, I waited in vain for a letter from Alexandre, gleaning every scrap of information I could from stagecoach drivers coming into Cadiz from Cordova, where I had last seen him, but gaining no hint of when I might expect to see him again. Fortunately our friend, M. de Saint-Prix, a young Frenchman who had traveled with us from Seville to Cadiz, promised to wait there till Alexandre arrived, and send him on with all speed to rejoin us later.

In spite of all these precautions to ensure the safe return of my prodigal son, it was with a heavy, anxious heart that I left Cadiz. It had been agreed that the *Véloce* would sail at eight o'clock in the morning of Saturday, November 21, and punctually at seven-thirty we were waiting on the quay to board the cutter that Commandant Bérard had sent to fetch us, while the ship's yawl, fully manned, took charge of our luggage.

The *Véloce* was surrounded by a great cloud of gulls of various kinds, and, moved by an impulse to give my future companions some idea of my skill as a marksman, I raised my gun and picked off two of the largest. Both fell, the crew of the yawl turned aside to retrieve them, and on this triumphant note we climbed aboard. As luck would have it,

4

both birds were merely stunned, so the surgeon clipped their wings with a pair of scissors and set them free on deck, where they immediately made themselves at home. The sailors, great boys that they are, at once adopted them as pets and christened them *Véloce* and *Achéron*, respectively, while Paul introduced a third gull, almost as large as an albatross, that we had captured on our trip down the Guadalquivir and had named *El Rapido*, in honor of the vessel we were on at that time.

Our first duty was to place our passports in the Captain's hands, and we hastened to observe this formality, the more quickly to relegate our official status to the background. Since the War Minister and the Minister of Foreign Affairs, speaking in the Tribune, have both disclaimed any knowledge of my being sent on an official mission, I must point out that my passport, issued by the Minister of State for Foreign Affairs, expressly stated that I was being sent on a mission by the Minister of Education, and was signed by *le chef de bureau de la chancellerie*, De Lamarre.[3] If the Minister of Foreign Affairs protests that he signs so many passports that he could very well have forgotten signing this particular one, I will add a personal detail to refresh his memory. M. Génie, writing on behalf of the Minister of Foreign Affairs, requested me to attend in person at the Ministry on October 2, 1846, at 11 A.M., to receive my passport. I did so, and was kept waiting for nearly two hours. If M. Guizot has forgotten this circumstance, M. de Salvandy, whose memory is more reliable, will certainly recall it.

In addition to Captain Bérard and Lieutenant Vial, of whom you have already heard, Madame, there were four other officers aboard the *Véloce;* the second lieutenant, the second sub-lieutenant,[4] the ship's surgeon and the paymaster. The

3. In the original text Dumas quoted his passport in full.—*Ed.*
4. The first sub-lieutenant, M. Durande, an experienced officer of mature age, was away on special duty in connection with the rescue of a group of French prisoners from the Arab chief, Abd-el-Kader. Cf. Ch. 7.—*Ed.*

second lieutenant, Monsieur Salles, was a man of about thirty-five, fair haired and kindly, very well informed and with delightful manners, but he was subject to bouts of depression due to ill health and would frequently shut himself in his cabin for hours on end, appearing only when actually on duty. By the time our trip was over we had almost cured him of his melancholy, if not of his illness, and I think he was sorry to lose us, if only because we took his mind off his troubles.

The second sub-lieutenant, Monsieur Antoine, was by no means young, and no one could say why promotion had passed him by, for he was considered an excellent officer by all his colleagues on board. Yet, in spite of his twenty years' service, since his rank did not entitle him to superannuation, he was still liable to be dismissed without pension at the whim of some petty government official. His precarious position worried him, making him either morose or very shy, and we saw little of him.

Monsieur Marquès, the senior surgeon, a young man of twenty-five or twenty-six, was acting as locum tenens for the regular ship's doctor, who was either on leave or absent through illness, I no longer remember which. M. Marquès was really an army doctor, and not yet accustomed to conditions afloat, so Maquet and Giraud were especially recommended to his sympathetic care.

The paymaster, Monsieur Rebec, came straight from Marseilles. He was actually born there, and I at once felt drawn to him as a kindred spirit. As you know, Madame, Marseilles is my second home. I have enjoyed such wonderful hospitality there, and some of my best friends, Méry, Autran, come from that city. When I wished to create two particular types of men, one showing human intelligence in the highest degree and the other portraying commercial integrity carried to extreme lengths, I borrowed them both from this daughter of old Phocaea whom I love as a mother, and called them Dantès and Morrel.

The rest of the ship's company, noncommissioned officers

and crew, totalled about 120 men, but we had no time for more than a superficial glance around, since the moment we came aboard the *Véloce* began to get under way. M. Vial's prophecy about the weather was quite wrong. Instead of the "set fair" he had promised us there was a fine rain casting a veil over Cadiz, that city of azure, emerald and gold, but he insisted that as soon as we were clear of the harbor the barometer would rise, the wind of the open sea would disperse the clouds, and before noon we should have our first sight of the strong sun and ever clear blue skies of Africa.

More than any other land in the world, Africa has magic in its very name. Old Homer will tell you that it was on Africa's enchanted shore that there grew the lotus whose sweet fruit caused travelers to lose even the memory of their native land—the strongest memory of all. It was in Africa that Herodotus placed the Garden of the Hesperides, whose fruit Hercules was to gather, and the Palace of the Gorgons, through whose great gates Perseus was to force his way. There, too, was the country of the Garamanthes, where, said Herodotus, the cattle were obliged to walk backward as they grazed because their great horns curved in front of their muzzles. In Africa, said Strabo, are leeches seven cubits long, big enough to drink the blood of twelve men; while, if you believe Pomponius Mela, Africa is the home of satyrs, fauns and strange beasts that dwell among the crags of lost Atlantis and howl to see the sun rise or set.

From Africa came travelers' tales of great, one-legged creatures that could outrun ostriches or gazelles; basilisks, whose breath would melt the hardest stone; dragons, prodigies and fabulous monsters. Pliny found nothing surprising in such reports, and put forward plausible reasons to explain why new species of animals were a natural result of conditions in Africa. In more recent times, it was in Algiers that Dr. Schaw[5]

5. Dumas was clearly referring to Dr. Thomas Shaw (1694–1751) F.R.S., a famous African traveler, born at Kendal in Westmoreland, the son of a wool-dyer. At the local grammar school he won a scholarship which took him to Queen's College, Oxford, where in later life

found his celebrated hybrid, called a Kumrah, the offspring of a cow and an ass. Only last year, in 1845, the scientific world in general, and Colonel Bory de Saint-Vincent in particular, acknowledged that a new variety of rodent, the horned rat, had been discovered in Africa—a charming little animal whose existence was suspected by Pliny, denied by M. Buffon, and has now been established beyond doubt by the Zéphyrs, Algeria's finest explorers.[6] So you see, Madame, from Homer's day to our own, Africa's magic has never ceased to fascinate travelers and philosophers. That mysterious land where, in Marco Polo's time, Prester John reigned over the

---

he became regius professor of Greek and principal of St. Edmund Hall. In 1720 he went out as chaplain to the English factory at Algiers, and during his thirteen years' residence there he closely studied the natural history of Algiers, Tripoli and Morocco, publishing the results of his research in Travels, or Observations relating to several parts of Barbary and the Levant (1742). In that work (Tome I, Part III, Ch. II, Sect. I, p. 166), Dr. Shaw, speaking of "the tame and wild quadrupeds," observes: "To the Mule we may join the Kumrah, as the Algerines call a little serviceable beast of burthen, begot between an Ass and a Cow. That which I saw at Algiers (where it was not looked upon as a rarity), was single-hoofed like the Ass, but distinguished from it in having a sleeker skin, with the tail and the head (though without horns) in fashion of the dam's."

Dr. Shaw's book, first translated into French and published at the Hague in 1743, was reissued in Paris in 1830, a version with which Dumas may well have been familiar.—Ed.

6. Dumas writes with apparently genuine enthusiasm and interest of this "discovery," which took place a few months before his visit. Either he was not aware of the outcome, or was writing here with his tongue in his cheek, for this celebrated "rat-à-trompe" was a hoax. (An account of the affair is contained in Le Larousse du XIXe siècle, p. 756.) A certain Zouave who occupied his over-abundant leisure in carrying out experiments on small mammals, managed to graft the severed tip of a rat's tail onto the nose of another rat so successfully that it seemed a natural development, like the horn of a rhinoceros. A visiting naturalist of some eminence was completely taken in, paid the Zouave a high price for this "new kind of desert rat," and was on the point of announcing his "discovery" to the scientific world when his suspicions were aroused and confirmed. Colonel Bory de Saint-Vincent, mentioned by Dumas, does not seem to have had any scientific qualifications and was probably concerned merely as the colonel of the corps known as the "Zéphyrs," to which the enterprising Zouave belonged.—Ed.

most fabulous kingdom the world has ever known, still remains an entrancing enigma. As for the places we live in, the more real they become to us, the sadder we know them to be.

At the moment, Madame, we are happily floating between these two vastly different worlds. Behind us, Europe is already vanishing in the rain; to port, as we say at sea, lies Gibraltar; and on the horizon ahead of us the mountains of Morocco are glinting in the sunshine. Maquet is already lying down in his cabin. Giraud can still keep upright, more or less, but he is muffled in his cloak, and so afraid of opening his mouth that he dare not utter a single word. Now and again he sits down, gloomy as Jeremiah on the banks of Jordan, obviously wishing he were with his family.

Desbarolles is striding up and down the deck with Vial, chatting and gesticulating as he tells of his travels in Spain, his hunting expeditions with the bandits of the Sierra Morena, his love affairs in Madrid, his encounters with the brigands of Villa Major and Malo Sitio. I notice that Desbarolles is careful to keep to windward of Vial's cigar, changing position each time they turn, and I fancy that before our voyage is over Desbarolles will feel a qualm or two of the trouble that has already laid Maquet low and is now threatening Giraud.

Boulanger and I, comfortably installed on a bench and holding on to the nearest rope, are swaying gently to counter the movement of the ship as she pitches and rolls, our whole attention absorbed by the subtle variations of color in the sea and sky. Most of the crew are off duty, sleeping, gossiping or amusing themselves with a game or two, while the twenty or twenty-five men we can see on deck are quietly busy around the capstan and the guns. Three midshipmen are playing with our pet gulls, which pounce on scraps of bread and strut around as happily as though they had never known any other life, while the *Véloce* forges steadily ahead, controlled only by the helmsman, who casually turns his wheel a point or two now and again. In this pleasant fashion we are being carried inexorably toward the unknown, drawing nearer every moment.

Vial was right. The sky is clearing and the sea is calmer now. There are strong currents flowing between the Atlantic and the Mediterranean Sea, but you will appreciate that such influences, though they would seriously embarrass a sailing ship, can be largely ignored by these new kings of the sea, that plow through their empire mounted on a throne of flame, wearing around their heads a crown of smoke.

People often talk about the tedium of sea travel. When the land has long vanished, and, day after day, as far as the eye can see there is nothing but sky and heaving waves, it is perhaps understandable if boredom, that companion or forerunner of malaise, sits constantly beside the voyager. But for a thinking man who tries to fathom the depths of meaning in the heavens and the ocean—those two symbols of infinity—I know of no sight more sublime than the horizon where clouds and waves lose themselves in each other.

I was lost in reverie when Vial, still walking and talking with Desbarolles, passed close to me, touched my shoulder, raised his arm and pointed out a headland where a sunbeam was striking through the rain. "Trafalgar!" he cried.

Some names possess a singular power and conjure up a whole train of thought. Between England and ourselves there are six words which epitomize all our history: Crécy, Poitiers, Agincourt, Aboukir, Trafalgar and Waterloo, each of them a defeat from which it seemed our country could never recover, a wound to drain the nation's very lifeblood. Yet France has never failed to rise again, with new strength flowing through her veins; every time England has come to our shores as a conquering invader we have repulsed her in the end. Joan of Arc won back the crown of France from Henry VI at Orléans; after Marengo and Austerlitz, Napoleon, at Amiens, reclaimed the fleurs-de-lis from George IV's coat of arms. True, the English burned Joan of Arc at the stake at Rouen and imprisoned Napoleon on Saint Helena, but we revenged ourselves by making her a holy martyr and him a god.

For five hundred years there has been this constant ebb and flow, this closely matched conflict, like Jacob's struggle with the angel in Genesis, or the ancient wars between Rome and Carthage. It may be that through the centuries England has prevailed by material force, France by spiritual strength, by her power to inspire all who love beauty and truth. If the flaming torch so long borne aloft by France were ever finally extinguished, a long cry of agony and despair would arise from the whole darkened world.

2

⚜ ⚜ ⚜

OFF TANGIER

At half-past six in the evening we cast anchor a mile or two off shore from Tangier, for dusk was already falling and it was too late to think of putting into port that night. As the movement of the ship died away, Giraud came down from his refuge on deck, Maquet ventured to leave his cabin, and when dinner was announced we all strolled comfortably along to the wardroom, our company once more complete, except for Alexandre.

It was the Captain's custom to invite each of his officers in turn to lunch or dine at his table, and on this occasion M. Vial was to dine with us. We were all in excellent spirits, and since none of our party, except Desbarolles and myself, had eaten since breakfast we all did full justice to the delicious meal. We had reached the dessert when we heard the officer of the watch give a hail, and soon afterward a message came down that the French *chancelier* at Tangier had arrived on board to welcome me, bringing with him an old friend of mine who was longing to shake my hand again in greeting.

Note that, Madame! I have said somewhere that I have thirty thousand friends up and down the world, and you see I was not exaggerating! There must be at least thirty thousand, if, in a place like Tangier, there is one, all agog to wait upon me in person the moment I arrive!

As we stood to receive the *chancelier*, our jaws dropped

and our eyes widened in astonishment, for behind him shone
the expansive, open countenance of Couturier! You must remember Couturier, Madame, our host in Granada on the day
we became involved in a regrettable fracas with the Con-
trairas family?[1] We had never set eyes on him since and
feared the earth must have swallowed him up, but he had
merely slipped out of Spain, and voluntarily at that! Knowing his skill with daguerreotypes, Monsieur Duchâteau had
offered him employment on the official visit to Morocco that
I spoke of earlier. Couturier had immediately gathered up his
paraphernalia and rushed off to Tangier, where the *Achéron*
was due to pick him up at any moment. He already knew
the town as well as he had known Granada, and would undertake to show us everything there was to see.

The *chancelier*, Monsieur Florat, also placed his services at
our disposal. Since the *Véloce* regularly visited Tangier, he
knew the Captain well, and had, indeed, been aware that the
ship had been sent to fetch me from Spain. When the *Véloce* was again sighted at anchor, the rumor of our arrival
spread through the town, and thus it was that Couturier had
managed to come and surprise us at a moment when, I must
confess, he was very far from our thoughts.

M. Florat was a very keen hunter, and as I had heard a
great deal about African hunting I asked him whether there
might be any way of arranging such an expedition in the
next day or two. He replied that to organize a hunting trip
into the interior was a highly complicated affair, especially
for Christians, but he would see what could be done, and
let us know. Boulanger and Maquet, who have never at any
time been any good with a gun, would prefer to wander
round the town with Couturier and produce wonders with a
pencil or a brush.

We all went up on deck together to take leave of our
visitors. The janissary[2] who had accompanied them on their

1. Cf. *Adventures in Spain*, Ch. 20.
2. A "janissary" originally meant "a soldier of the old Turkish Foot
Guards," a corps founded in 1330 and composed of renegade prisoners

outward journey stood waiting to escort them back, a cudgel in one hand, a lighted lantern in the other. Members of the consular service are doubtless inviolable, like diplomats and delegates, and could presumably dispense with a janissary, but in point of fact they never do. This particular one looked extremely disreputable, and though these gentlemen evidently trusted him to protect them, they would certainly not have considered him clean enough to be employed as a servant. But that is how things are in Morocco. For the rest, I know him to be very brave, and if ever you go to Tangier, Madame, I beg you to seek him out and make him your bodyguard. His name is El-Arbi-Bernat; he has only one eye; and should these details fail to identify him for you, here is a further clue. In his spare time he is an executioner.

Our visitors were anxious not to delay their return. As a representative of the French government, M. Florat had power to order the gates of the town to be opened for him at any hour, but he preferred not to exercise this authority, and left us at nine. (Force of habit almost made me say "as nine o'clock was striking," forgetting that here, in Africa, the hours, months, years, slip by without a sound.) The night was dark and overcast, save for a few stars shining in the sky and reflected in the ocean depths. We could not see the surface of the water, and our ship, like Mahomet's tomb, seemed suspended in space, so that as our friends went over the side they appeared to descend into a bottomless gulf. Soon, however, their lantern shone steadily over their tiny craft and the water around it, lighting up the flashing eyes and bare arms of the Moroccan oarsmen. Then the boat darted away from the ship's side like a swallow from a roof, her passengers still visible for a while in the circle of light, but the circle grew smaller and smaller till it looked to us like a star moving slowly toward the shore. At last it stopped,

---

and children taken as a tribute levied on Christian parents. The janissaries were disbanded after a revolt in 1826, but the term long remained in use with the meaning of a bodyguard employed to protect a traveler from attack.—*Ed.*

flickered erratically this way and that like a will-o'-the-wisp, mounted a slope, disappeared, shone out again and suddenly vanished as though the earth had swallowed it up. The gates of Tangier had just closed behind M. Florat and his companion.

We noticed with surprise that Tangier itself was the blackest spot in the whole coast line. Behind us, on the far side of the bay, shone the fires of the outcast Arabs who lie hidden by day in the scrub that fringes the mountains. Now and then the howling of jackals and hyenas re-echoed almost like human voices across the water; but in Tangier, a town of seven thousand people, there was not a sound, not one chink of light. It lay dark and silent as a tomb.

How strange it is, I thought to myself! You are perfectly at home anywhere in Europe, but if you cross this narrow stretch of water to Africa, you are at once conscious of a fundamental change. This morning you left a friendly country, but tonight you are in a hostile land. Those fires you see were lit by men of a race alien to your own, who regard you as their enemy though you have done them no harm; the cries you hear are uttered by wild animals unknown in your own country, roaming like the lion of the Scriptures, seeking whom they may devour. Once you set foot in that land, even if you evade the wild beasts, how shall you escape the enmity of man?

So I stood musing until Vial came to remind me there would be no moon to bring me light, and at last I went below. I awoke as the men of the morning watch were beginning to scrub the deck, and, fully refreshed, I dressed and went out. It was the moment when darkness still resisted the dawn, and the great semicircular bay seemed a lake of molten silver framed by black mountains. On one side, the tower that crowns Cape Malabata was faintly outlined against the first pale light of morning; on the other, flanked by Cape Spartel, I could just distinguish Tangier, lying fast asleep on the shore. Here and there in the mountains fires were flickering, and in the sky a few last stars still twinkled. After a while, a faint rosy mist glided from the east along the strait between Europe and Africa, shedding a wonderfully gentle, translucent light as it moved along the coast of Spain from the Sierra de San Matéo to Cape Trafalgar, whitening the villages and isolated dwellings scattered along the seaboard.

The sun had not yet risen, but its bright rays were already striking upward behind the mountains that ringed us round. Slowly the light grew stronger, its beams merging into an immense globe of fire, and at the very moment when this shining orb lifted its rim above Cape Malabata (which itself remained in blue shadow), the eastern slope of Cape Spartel suddenly glowed with a golden brightness, lifting Tangier out of darkness and casting the shadow of its chalk-white buildings between the yellow shore and the verdant crest of the opposing hill. Where sunbeams ran over the waves, the sea itself grew pink, though in the shadows its color was still a pale sulphur or the cold tint of lead. At last, the sun rose like a conqueror to command the heavens, and a new day had begun. At that very moment a caravan of a dozen camels, seven or eight mules and five or six donkeys came out of a mountain gorge in single file and wound its way like a serpent along the sand, making for Tangier.

Less fortunate than the caravan, we Christians would not be allowed to enter Tangier till later in the day, so the Commandant asked if we would like a morning's fishing. The sea was free to all, and we could doubtless beat off any attack from the shore. You can imagine how the idea appealed to us, Madame, and also to the crew of the *Véloce*, for Captain Bérard offered to send with us every man who could be spared from the ship. For the sailors it was a double pleasure—they looked forward to the sport and also to bringing back a harvest of fish to supplement their normal fare. Almost instantly their boat was launched and the nets prepared. We were to go in the yawl with M. Vial, who was in charge of the expedition; Maquet and Rebec came too, and each of us carried a double-barreled musket. The men in the fishing boat had a dozen carbines, and, should it prove to be necessary, the *Véloce* would use her guns to defend us.

As we were going down the starboard ladder we noticed a boat being rowed swiftly toward us, signaling frantically. Clearly it had some urgent business with the *Véloce*, so we waited to learn what this might be. When the little craft drew nearer we recognized El-Arbi-Bernat, the janissary who had come aboard the night before, and as soon as he came within hailing distance he explained to me in halting Spanish that M. Florat, using his telescope on the high balcony of the consulate, had seen us preparing to go fishing, and since the shore would be swarming with Arabs on their way to market he had sent us his own bodyguard. Proud and happy to be entrusted with this mission, El-Arbi-Bernat settled himself in our bow; the bosun's pipe gave a signal; the oars, till now vertical and motionless, swept down to strike the water in perfect unison, and the yawl, heading the convoy, began moving toward the shore.

I mentioned earlier that the *Véloce* frequently put in to Tangier, and Vial was therefore familiar with the bay. He steered toward the mountain where I had seen the night fires burning, and I inquired its name. It was the Scharff, and at its foot, to the right of Old Tangier, the river Oued-Echak flowed into the sea. We made for this opening and went up-stream as far as we could, but the tide was falling, our heavily loaded craft was drawing nearly three feet of water, so before long she grounded, and perforce we stopped. We had made no attempt to land at any other point, for though the sea was calm enough further out there were strong breakers all along the shore, and we should have risked capsizing. Now, two sailors jumped overboard without even bothering to roll up their trousers, and put their shoulders together to form a seat on which Vial, then the rest of us in turn, rode comfortably to the river bank. The yawl, lightened by this maneuver, was refloated and steered further up the river till she grounded once more. This time she could be safely left, for the water level was falling rapidly and would not sweep her out to sea again.

17

As for the larger craft manned by the *matelots*, she had no need to take such precautions, and had sailed straight to the nearest point of land. A short distance off shore, the sailors had dived overboard like cormorants and thrust their boat through the breakers till she was well up on the sand.

At this moment a sea swallow flew by. I fired, and the wounded bird fell on the further bank of the river. As I walked toward the stream, debating whether it was worth getting wet to retrieve such poor game, the barrel of a long gun rose above the crest of a dune, followed by the hood of a burnoose, a bronze-colored head, and the body of a bare-legged Arab. Clearly he had assumed that the shot he had heard was fired by one of his fellow countrymen, and on seeing us he halted.

I had never seen an Arab before, except in the paintings of Delacroix and Vernet, or in sketches by Raffet or De-camps, and I was profoundly impressed by this living example of an African race that had risen from the earth before me and was now standing motionless thirty paces away, his gun over his shoulder and one foot forward, like a statue of Circumspection. Had I been alone he would have thought nothing of my musket with its eighteen-inch barrel—his own gun was five feet long—but behind me there were fifty men of my own race, clad as I was, and our numbers gave him pause.

We might have stood there, one on each side of this new Rubicon, till the Day of Judgment, so I called to El-Arbi-Bernat to ask the Arab to come across and bring my swallow with him. After the exchange of a few brief phrases he did so without hesitation, and as he forded the river he carefully examined the swallow, which had a broken wing and a pellet of lead in its breast. He gave me the bird without speaking and went on his way, but as he passed Bernat he asked him a question or two. I inquired what he had said, and Bernat replied:

"He asked whether you had shot that bird in flight. I told him I had seen you do so."

"Was that when I saw him shake his head in doubt?" I persisted. "Did he not believe you, then?"

"Not more than he could help."

"Do you know him? Is he a good marksman?"

"Yes. He is considered one of the best shots hereabouts."

"Call him back, then."

The Arab rejoined us surprisingly quickly, obviously curious to have a closer look at us, or rather our guns, and halted five paces from me. Giraud and Boulanger, who had been following him with their sketch books and pencils in hand, stopped too. He was the first Arab they, like myself, had ever seen, and from their eagerness to commit him to paper you would have thought they never expected to see another.

"Here is a Frenchman," said Bernat to the Arab, "who fancies he can shoot better than you." A little smirk of incredulity curled his hearer's lips, and Bernat continued, "He shot this bird as it flew, and doubts whether you could do as much."

"I can do the same."

"Very well. By a lucky chance here comes another bird. Quick! Kill it!" But the Arab made no move except to reply: "The Frenchman did not kill his with a bullet."

"What does he say?" I asked, and when I knew I went on: "That's very true. Here is some lead for him," and I poured out a charge of number-five shot. He still shook his head and spoke a few words. I looked inquiringly at Bernat. "He says that powder is dear, and there are too many hyenas and panthers about for him to waste powder on birds."

"Tell him I will give him six charges of powder for every round he shoots against me." The janissary conveyed my offer to the Arab, who stood silent and thoughtful while Boulanger and Giraud went on with their sketches. Clearly the Arab was weighing the value of twenty or thirty charges of powder against the risk to his own reputation, but cupidity won. He removed the bullet from his gun, stretched out his palm for some powder, reloaded, examined the trigger carefully, and stood waiting.

19

He had not long to wait, for this part of the African coast abounds in game. A plover passed overhead. The Arab took long and careful aim before he fired, but the bird sailed on without losing a single feather. At the sound of the shot a snipe flew up, and as it came within range I brought it down. The Arab gave me a half-smile. "The Frenchman shoots well," he said, "but a real hunter shoots with a bullet, not small shot." As Bernat translated I replied: "That's perfectly true. I quite agree with him. Let him choose a target for himself, anything he likes, and I will match him."

"First of all, the Frenchman owes me six charges of powder," said the Arab, stretching out his hand. I poured into it about a third of my store, and watched while he carefully let it run into his own powder horn, from the first grain to the very last, with a skill and concentration that roused my respect. That done, he seemed inclined to move on, but our artists had not quite completed their portraits, so I spoke to Bernat again.

"Remind your countryman that he and I both have a bullet to dispose of. Let him fix whatever mark he likes." "I agree," returned the Arab, picking up a thin piece of driftwood and looking round for something else. In my pocket I had a letter from one of my nephews who is employed in His Majesty's private household. Its large square envelope and red seal seemed to me to meet our needs exactly, so I passed it to the Arab, who understood at once. Splitting the end of the spar with his knife he inserted the envelope, thrust the stick into the sand and strode slowly back toward us counting twenty-five paces. Then he reloaded his gun. My own double-barreled musket, an excellent weapon from Devisme, the best gunsmith in Paris, was already loaded with those new pointed bullets that can kill a man at fifteen hundred meters. I took it from Paul, its usual custodian, and stood waiting. The Arab took aim with a care that proved his determination not to be beaten a second time. He fired, one corner of the envelope vanished, and in spite of his traditional self-control he uttered a cry of joy before turning to see what I could do.

"Tell him," I instructed Bernat, "that in France we like to be further from our target," and my opponent watched in amazement while I paced out twice the distance. "Now," I continued, "explain that my first bullet will hit the target near the red seal, and my second will break the stick." Having announced this program I took aim with the utmost precision I was capable of, for it was my duty to carry out my declared intention. It would not do to come to Africa and mislead the natives, but fortunately I did not default. My first bullet hit the seal, and almost simultaneously my second shattered the spar.

The Arab flung his gun across his shoulder and stalked off without a word, not even waiting for the charges of powder I owed him. His defeat was a severe blow to his self-respect, and I doubt if he looked around, or even raised his head, till he reached Tangier. Two or three other Arabs passing along the shore had stopped to watch, and now moved silently onward, equally downcast. All Morocco had been humiliated in the person of one of her sons.

Meanwhile our fishermen had been busy, and were now pulling in the net. To fish with a net is the most moving of all methods. The number of people needed to manage it, the circle it forms, the uncertainty of the catch—all these combine to produce an excitement that I can understand far better than an enthusiasm for rod and line, notwithstanding the opportunity that sport gives for a singlehanded contest between man and fish. While our men, in water up to their necks, were coping with the net and shouting encouragingly to each other, the shore, deserted when we landed, was becoming crowded with Arabs on their way from the neighboring *goums* to the market in Tangier to sell their produce.

But what sellers they were, and what a strange impression they gave of African commerce! One was a charcoal vendor, who carried in each hand one or two pieces of blackened

21

wood. Another had ten or twelve bricks to sell; a third sold poultry, and was driving along a young turkey with a stick, carrying a couple of pigeons on his arm and a hen hanging at his back. One or two had a tiny donkey loaded with wood or vegetables, but these were men of considerable importance in Moroccan commercial circles, who might take home as much as twenty sous if they sold all their wares. For the majority, two or three sous would have been ample payment for the goods they carried, yet they came from four, six, or even ten leagues around, bringing with them their whole families: their wives, wearing huge hats of plaited rushes, their faces hidden from view; children clinging to their mothers' hands or carried on their backs to supplement their burdens of bricks or fowls; old, white-bearded men walking with sticks or riding on donkeys like patriarchs on their way to some modern Jerusalem.

Yet, in spite of their rags and their poverty, all of them moved with a superb dignity. For them, dignity dwells in the man himself, not in his rank or the clothes he wears. An Arab is a sultan in his own home, and if, by his biweekly visits to Tangier to sell his produce, he can gain enough to keep his family until the next market day, he asks nothing more of life. He has no higher ambition.

For the most part they passed by without pausing, without even glancing in our direction. A few stopped to ask our janissary a question or two, and Giraud and Boulanger took the opportunity to sketch them. Two or three resented that their likeness was thus filched from them, and went on their way grumbling fiercely. Others, generally the younger ones, were keenly interested in the drawings, and laughed uproariously to see themselves thus represented on paper. Among all these men, only three or four at most were armed, and with very inferior guns. They had no other weapons that I saw. On the far side of the bay, camel and mule trains, shrunk by distance to the size of ants, continued to make their way to Tangier.

Already the net had been thrown twice, and the catch,

though not poor, was by no means miraculous. While the sailors prepared for a third attempt, and Giraud and Boulanger were busy with their sketchbooks, Maquet, Vial and I strolled along the shore in search of game. Paul came with us to serve as interpreter. (Chevet[3] was perfectly right. Paul was a true Arab, and except for slight differences of local dialect we found he could understand everyone we met.) After an hour or so, during which we had picked up three or four plovers and half a dozen snipe, we saw the signal for our return run up on the mainmast of the *Véloce*. It had been agreed that this signal would be hoisted between ten and eleven o'clock to let us know that *déjeuner* would shortly be served, and we immediately began to round up the crew, who had four great buckets full of most appetizing-looking fish.

It was by no means easy to return to the boats. The sailors, who had been soaked to the skin for three hours, made short work of the breakers; Vial, being carried out, was engulfed by a wave, while Maquet and I swam out. Boulanger, taking advantage of a temporary lull, arrived on board dry shod; Desbarolles and Giraud escaped with a few splashes, and soon we were being rowed back to the *Véloce*.

There an excellent meal awaited us, and two guests had already arrived to do justice to it—M. Florat and Couturier. We lunched in some haste, for we were anxious to get to Tangier before the market closed at one o'clock, but there is no private house, no matter how exalted, where the service is as speedy and well organized as on a ship of the line, and in a surprisingly short time we were ready to leave. The fishing boat was dancing at the foot of the ladder; in an instant we had settled ourselves in her; the oars swept down, and we were moving swiftly toward Tangier.

3. M. Chevet recommended Dumas to employ Paul as his personal servant. Cf. *Adventures in Spain*, Ch. 2.—*Ed*.

3

❧ ❧ ❧

THE MARKET IN TANGIER

The eye of a stranger approaching Tangier from the sea is first drawn to the quarter where the consulates stand grouped together, each flying the flag of its own country: England, Spain, Portugal, Holland, Sweden, Sardinia, Naples, the United States, Denmark, Austria and France. In the rest of the town only two buildings overtop the roof gardens of the uniform, single-story dwellings: the Casbah and the mosque—the palace of the Sultan and the house of God. As we landed, the muezzin was calling the faithful to prayer, his voice full, sonorous and commanding, befitting a religion sprung from the sword.

The harbor itself was almost empty, except for two or three Spanish vessels loading up, their crews talking with the Moroccans in Sabir, an odd mixture of Greek, Italian and French that will take you anywhere around the Mediterranean coast. A score of Arab porters on the jetty were dismantling an old boat. In their midst, obviously awaiting us, stood a man of middle height, aged about thirty-five or forty, with strongly marked features, quick, intelligent eyes and shaven head. He wore a black skull cap and a long coat of the same color, tied at the waist with what must once have been a handsome sash, though now rather tattered. He handed us ashore, then with an air of authority (softened for the bystanders by a kindly smile from M. Florat), he placed himself at the head of our column and marched forward,

24

calling, "Make way! Make way!" A corps of the Moroccan Guard that happened to be on our route, seeing us so ceremoniously conducted, took us for persons of some importance and saluted us as they passed.

Tangier still claims to be a warlike stronghold, but her fortifications are now crumbling, and here and there lie open to the sky. At the head of the ramp leading up from the shore stands the town gate, low and massive under its pointed arch, guarded by a ragged soldier carrying a musket with a gold-chased barrel and a butt inlaid with ivory. The gate leads to a rough and narrow street, bordered by whitewashed houses with no openings on to the thoroughfare except their doors. Now and then I saw a great niche hollowed out in the middle of a house wall, and in it a man wrapped in a white burnoose or enveloped in a blanket, lying smoking with such gravity and detachment that not for anything in the world would I have disturbed him. Yet, to judge from the shapeless bundles beside him and the balance by his feet, he was a fruit-seller, a grocer or a butcher. Other men were leaning comfortably against a wall, enjoying the November sun, or sitting cross-legged with their heads thrown back, silently telling their prayer beads. Now and again a figure crouching on a house top rose and climbed over to the next roof—an Arab woman calling on her neighbor.

As we approached the center of the town we could hear the roar of the market in full swing, but M. Florat was unable to take us to visit it himself. At the door of the French consulate he halted, saying to the man in the black coat: "You quite understand, David. I am trusting these gentlemen to your care." Turning to us he added: "My friends, ask David for anything you want." David bowed, we gestured to show our thanks, and so it was settled between us. Then, taking me aside, M. Florat whispered: "This man, David Azercot, is a Jew, a marine store dealer. If, by any chance, you were to present him with a draft for a hundred thousand francs, he would pay it at sight, probably in gold. Au revoir. I shall see you at the consulate before long."

I turned back to David with heightened interest. So here was a real, traditional Levantine Jew. With us, the Jew is no longer a distinct type. He has merged with the rest of society, with nothing in his speech, appearance or dress to distinguish him from other men. He can be an officer of the Legion of Honour, an Academician, a baron, a prince, even a king! In England, too, the Jews have an important place in the commercial life of the nation, and are respected for their integrity. But the further one gets from the center of civilization, the more submissive and fearful, the more oppressed, are the Jews. In Tangier, for example, Jews are forced to remove their shoes when they pass in front of the mosque. However, thanks to his official position as a contractor to the navy, David Azercot was allowed special privileges, and the one he valued most was the right to walk past the mosque in his blue socks and laced shoes. Indeed, he took us a long way round so that we should actually see him enjoying this concession. Poor man! Perhaps he would have paid dearly for this strange prerogative if we had not bombarded Tangier and won the battle of Isly![1]

At last we arrived at our goal, and found there all the sellers of charcoal, wood and poultry that we had met on the seashore. I have no idea who was the first to call the Arabs grave and silent. Grave, yes; but silent, no! There is nothing so noisy as an Arab market, and the uproar at this one was enough to make one's head split! All around the crowd was a great circle of camels and mules, almost as grave as their owners and far more silent, except that occasionally a camel would stretch out his long, snaky neck and utter a high-pitched scream, quite unlike the sound made by any other animal.

Giraud and Boulanger, in a frenzy of delight, settled themselves in the midst of sellers of dates and figs and covered their albums with sketches, each more picturesque than the

1. The victory of the Isly, August, 1844, was won by forces commanded by Thomas Robert Bugeaud, who was Governor of Algeria during Dumas' visit.—*Ed.*

last. I noticed that these fruits, and, indeed, all food stuffs, were offered to us Europeans at prices beyond all reason. We came across the cook from the *Véloce* bargaining for some red partridges. They cost four sous each, and he indignantly complained that the country was getting worse every day. At that rate it would soon be beyond bearing.

The market closed at one o'clock, and ten minutes later was completely deserted, except for little naked children searching among the debris for a fig or a raisin. For some time I had been asking David to take me to a bazaar where I could buy the things travelers generally bring back from a trip to North Africa—sashes, burnooses, *haiks*,[2] but he always replied in his gentle voice with its slight Italian accent, "I can sell you goods like that, monsieur. Shall we go to my place?" till at last I gave in and agreed.

Writing now, at a distance, Madame, I can give you no idea where his house was. Anyway, the Moors have no idea of how to name their streets properly! I remember that we went down through the market place, took a little alley leading off to the right, climbed a slope where the cobbles were all slippery with water from a fountain, and at last came to a locked door on which David knocked in a peculiar fashion. It was opened by a woman of about thirty years, her head bound with a turban, as in Biblical times—Madame Azercot. Facing the street door was an inner gateway where two or three young girls were crowding shyly together, and beyond was the usual little square courtyard with a flight of stairs against one wall, leading up to a gallery. Around this gallery were several rooms, and one of them was a kind of curiosity shop where sashes of every imaginable hue, *haiks* in almost incredible variety, silken cushions, carpets with myriad colors, were piled on tables, flung over the arms of chairs, or strewn across the floor. On the walls hung pouches and game bags of morocco leather, sabers of beaten copper, silver daggers. Every corner was heaped high with fine knee boots,

2. *Haik:* a large piece of woolen or cotton cloth worn by the Arabs over the tunic but under the burnoose.—*Ed.*

slippers embroidered in gold and silver, and innumerable *che-chias*, the traditional red caps that Zouaves wear, while above this confusion swung old-fashioned firearms with long barrels of unpolished iron and silver-mounted stocks studded with coral.

Maquet and I stood for a moment, lost in amazement at the treasures around us. (Giraud and Boulanger were no longer with us. They had gone with Paul and the janissary to visit the Casbah.) David waited silently beside us, still as patient and obsequious as though all these riches were some other man's possessions. I felt in my pockets, where the very coins were trembling with fright, and I dared not inquire the cost of even one of the things around me! They seemed worth a king's ransom! At last I timidly ventured to ask the price of a sash of white silk, striped with broad bands of gold. "Forty francs!" replied David. It took my breath away, and he had to repeat it twice! It was a real bargain, but, Madame, there is a true proverb that says: "Bargains can ruin a man more quickly than anything else," and certainly I found it so! Once I began asking prices I had to have an example of everything! Worse still, I went on to inquire for things that were not on show but which I remembered seeing in private collections or in paintings—finely chased copper vessels, mother-of-pearl caskets, tobacco jars of strange, Eastern design, Turkish *chibouques*, hookahs, anything that came into my head, and every time David, patient and humble as ever, went away for five minutes and came back with whatever I had asked him for, till I was almost panic-stricken to see my wishes taking shape before me in this fashion.

My thoughts turned to my friends, who at this moment were doubtless being baked by the heat in the courtyard of the Casbah. I suddenly recalled a lovely painting of a Jewess that I had seen in the studio of Delacroix after his return from Morocco, and I thought what a treat it would be to my companions to have a similar model. It was, however, a delicate matter to suggest on first acquaintance, and

I hesitated to mention it to David, but he immediately perceived that there was some desire in my mind and pressed me to name it.

"My dear David, I should probably be asking the impossible."

"Who knows? Tell me, anyway."

"One of my close friends, a great artist, came to Tangier about twelve years ago with another friend of mine, the Count of Mornay."

"Ah, yes! It was M. Delacroix."

"What? You know Delacroix, David?"

"He did me the honor to visit my poor house."

"Well! He painted a little picture of a Jewess wearing the loveliest traditional robes."

"I know. That was my sister-in-law Rachel."

"Is she still living, David? Would she agree to sit for my friends Giraud and Boulanger as she did for Delacroix? She was wonderfully beautiful."

"God has spared her to us, monsieur, but she is fifteen years older now."

"That's not of the least consequence, David. Will you persuade her to agree?"

"Sir, I think I can offer you a better model—my cousin Molly, who happens to be staying with us. But your friends will have to be quick, for she lives at Tarifa and may be going home tomorrow. Go and find your two companions— I will send a guide to take you to the Casbah—and when you come back Molly will be waiting for you, dressed as Rachel was."

"This is wonderful, David. You are an amazing man."

"I do what I can, and wish I could do more, since it was M. Florat who asked me to look after you," he replied, and before I could recover from my surprise he had called his brother to conduct me to the Casbah.

As we entered the courtyard where Giraud and Boulanger were busily sketching, an old Moorish woman was raising her arms toward heaven with a gesture of despair, uttering a few words of prayer or threats so vehemently that I asked David's brother what she was saying. It was: "Oh, God! How deeply we must have offended Thee, since Thou dost permit these dogs of Christians to come and draw in the Emperor's palace!" Not a polite invocation, but the Moors have never been celebrated for their hospitality and I paid her no further attention but went straight to our two artists who were just finishing their sketches. "Come quickly," I called to them. "There is a wonderful model waiting for you at David's house." Fortunately, they are in the habit of following my suggestions without hesitation, and five minutes later we were back in the room I had just left. As we entered, we all broke into a spontaneous cry of admiration and delight. On the low couch, now cleared of all the shining silks that had lately covered it, sat an adorable Jewish girl, glowing with youth and beauty, resplendent in robes decked with rubies, sapphires, diamonds. You may already have seen her portrait, engraved by Geoffroy from Boulanger's drawing and given the title "Molly," a far from Jewish name.

4

❦   ❦   ❦

A DAY'S HUNTING

At the very moment when Giraud and Boulanger were putting the finishing touches to their portraits, and poor Molly had been posing for them for two or three hours with the patience of an angel, M. Florat appeared on the gallery outside, having come to take us to the Chancellery.

On our way we became aware of a strange noise that grew louder as we approached a certain house—a noise like the surf on the pebbles at Dieppe, the buzzing of a million bees, the croaking of innumerable frogs—and, drawn by curiosity, we craned our necks through the doorway. It was a Moorish school, a primitive place with no paper, ink or pen, containing merely the first essentials for a school, a master and pupils. The master was sitting cross-legged against a wall, holding a stick long enough to reach the furthest corner of the room. The scholars sat around him in a semicircle, also cross-legged, each with an Arab rosary in hand. They were learning by heart a few verses from the Koran, their sole education. A man who knows twenty verses has reached graduation level; if he knows fifty he ranks as a Bachelor of Science; a man who knows a hundred is a *taleb*, and a *taleb* is a very learned man, who may hope to earn a living writing messages for less literate citizens, or telling stories to amuse customers in cafés.

When a pupil faltered or made an error he felt the master's stick, and a shriller note intruded upon the general hum. We

31

could have spent some time in studying this model school, but the master, fearing perhaps that the glances of Christians might have some undesirable influence upon the young believers in his charge, sent one of his pupils to shut the door in our faces. The door itself, we noticed with surprise, was really beautiful, much nicer to look at than this frightful school and its poor little scholars with their spindle legs and swollen, misshapen heads. It was of cedar, hewn into a high-pointed Moorish arch and studded with great copper nails. The spaces between these nails were filled with a profusion of intricate designs outlined by thousands of tiny sprigs, and, strangely enough, the emblems which recurred most frequently were the cross and the fleur-de-lis, the two symbols which, for eight hundred years, have marked the encroachment of the West upon the East. We spent some time admiring it and making a sketch or two before going on our way to the consul's residence.

M. Duchâteau, as I had learned at Cadiz, was away on a good-will mission to the Emperor Abd-el-Rhaman with gifts from King Louis-Philippe, and M. Roche had accompanied him, but we were charmingly welcomed by their unofficial deputies, Madame Roche and Mademoiselle Florence Duchâteau, who were delighted to receive visitors from France. It must be a hard penance for a *Parisienne* to be exiled to Tangier which is by no means a fashionable town!

M. Florat had told them how much we hoped to take part in a boar hunt, and they had been good enough to set matters in train. Does it surprise you, Madame, that members of your own, gentler, sex should concern themselves with arranging a hunting expedition? You must remember that one cannot go hunting near Tangier in the free and easy way one does around Saint-Denis. Extremely delicate diplomatic negotiations are involved, and no man can equal the ladies when it comes to delicate diplomatic negotiations!

Everything depended upon the English consul, Mr. Hay, an enthusiastic hunter who has won considerable local esteem by popularizing his favorite sport and organizing every event of this kind for miles around. Now, everyone in Tangier who owns a sporting gun looks to him for the chance to use it. No stranger can go hunting at all, unless he is in Mr. Hay's party or carries a permit signed by him. We, unfortunately, could not hunt in his company, for Mr. Hay was suffering from a sprain, so it was a question of obtaining his permission. Mme Roche and Mlle Duchâteau had called on Mr. Hay to plead our cause, with such success that he had not only signed a permit for us but had been kind enough to instruct his senior assistant to come with us, a Mr. Saint-Leger, almost as famous a hunter as his chief, who offered us a choice of dates. We decided upon the very next day, and inscribed our thanks to our hostesses in their albums, Maquet, Desbarolles and I in verse, Giraud and Boulanger in a couple of sketches, before returning to the *Véloce* for dinner.

I must tell you, Madame, that there is no restaurant in Tangier. In Spain, as I discovered, meals are poor and scanty, but in Morocco one has no meals at all. Now and then the inhabitants nibble a fig or a date, drink a cup of coffee, smoke a *chibouque*, and take nothing more for twenty-four hours, unless they join in the nightly revels that take place around fountains like the one near David's house. No fountain running with wine at some royal celebration ever roused such transports of joy as those we witnessed in Tangier, where men crowd together till midnight to drink fresh water. It is the same in all torrid zones, where the chief source of life is not the sun, as with us, but water. Wherever there is a river, a tiny stream or a spring, life puts forth shoots and grows. Only water can bring green to grass and trees, liveliness to animals and gaiety to men. What was the greatest miracle wrought by Moses? Bringing forth a gushing stream from the rock at a touch from his rod!

At five o'clock next morning we were afoot, our weapons already prepared for us by the gunnery officer. Giraud and Boulanger had decided to come with us after all, having realized that they might just as well sketch one of our thirty or forty Arab beaters in action as a beggar or hermit squatting against a wall in Tangier. While we were on board, surrounded by all the familiar comforts of civilization, Tangier seemed a thousand miles away, until we went on deck. There before us in the early light lay this town of contrasts, where, hidden among the houses that could boast of nothing more than a piece of rush matting within their four white-washed walls, there was, as we remembered, a certain Jewish home as full of treasures as a bazaar in *The Thousand and One Nights*.

Eight sturdy oarsmen rowed us to the quay, where David was waiting for us. The evening before, when we had begun to inquire about some means of transport, David had, by a gesture, relieved us of any concern, and now that amazing man had twelve horses and twelve Arab grooms waiting for us outside his house, completely blocking the street, which, like most thoroughfares in Tangier, was only six or eight feet wide. Ten minutes later we were joined by M. Florat and Mr. Saint-Leger. I was very surprised to see that Mr. Saint-Leger wore no hat, in spite of the sun, and his legs above his ankle boots were bare to the knees. When I ventured to ask him about it, he told me the story of how Diogenes threw away his wooden bowl when he saw a child drink from his hand. Saint-Leger had noticed the Arabs going bare-legged and Negroes with their heads uncovered, and had decided to do the same. As a final gesture of defiance to the equatorial sun, he wore his hair cut very short, *en brosse*. For the rest, he was one of the most friendly men I have ever known, and was familiar with every detail of the country around Tangier. We each bestrode a horse and rode along side by side.

Each man of our party was attended by a *sais* who ran beside his horse and carried his gun. M. Florat's attendant was a huge Negro from the Congo, whose face, even after allowing for his racial characteristics, seemed singularly lacking in intelligence. It was obvious from the way they treated him that the Moorish servants considered him as far beneath them as they themselves were below the Europeans of the party. Oppression had forced the Moors into subservience; they in turn oppressed the Negro, who finally was carrying everyone's burden without daring to utter the slightest protest. Bowed under his load he staggered on in his single cotton robe, without having even one hand free to wipe away the streams of sweat shining on his soot-black face.

For two hours we marched on through country that surprised me, for the valleys we followed were emerald green with stiff, sharp-edged grass as tall as a man's thigh, and flocks of plovers and red grouse flew up as we passed. Then, on the crest of a mountain outlined against the clear blue sky, we caught sight of a group of Arabs, thirty or so, standing leaning on their long guns, waiting for us. We signaled to them, their chief waved his burnoose in response, and we began to climb the mountain, whose narrow, stony paths, shrubs and stunted trees reminded me very much of the Sierra Morena. The sure-footed way our mounts climbed the stony mountain side, with its slope of forty-five degrees, proved their Arab ancestry, though they looked the roughest kind of hacks. Nobility always leaves some trace, and where French horses would have fallen twenty times, these Moroccan animals never once stumbled.

On the mountaintop we came up to the Arabs, who had not moved a step to meet us. Mr. Saint-Leger spoke to them and was given some recognition, though they were grave and polite, like men obeying an order rather than sharing a pleasure. (M. Florat assured me that if Mr. Hay had been there instead of Mr. Saint-Leger, they would have been as cordial as now they were cold.) After a brief exchange of civilities we moved on, for we still had a couple of miles to cover before the hunt could begin. It was almost impossible to discern any track on the mountain side, densely covered as it was with myrtles, lentish and arbutus trees tall enough to overtop horse and rider, and I could not understand how we should ever manage to get through such a thickset forest. Our chief guide was an old white-bearded, bare-legged Arab, whose gun, originally a matchlock, had in course of time been altered to a wheel lock and then to a flintlock. A hundred years from now, one of his descendants will have made it into a percussion musket. At last he brought us to an open stretch of ground strewn with boulders, where, later on, we should have our midday meal. The sun beat fiercely down and there was no shade at all, except close against the rocks which were too hot to touch, but out from a spring below them flowed a little stream that seemed all the cooler and sweeter in contrast with the furnace above it.

On we went into a shallow wooded valley, the spot chosen for the first *battue*. In my opinion, it was an impossible place to hunt in, for one could see no further than ten paces, and there was no protection from a wounded beast except tufts of arbutus that he would thrust aside like grass. Still, we took our positions as instructed and the shouting began. I have listened to shouts from a good many beaters in my time, but never any as fierce as these. They were yells, howls, imprecations that grew in ferocity as the beaters worked themselves into a state of wild exaltation. Paul was standing behind me with my second gun, and I asked him what their cries meant. He told me they were rounding up a wild boar lying in a thicket, and shouting to it: "Get out of there, you Jew!" Two or three of the men who had come with us bringing hired horses were Jews, and the Arab beaters were taking this opportunity of venting their spite against them, possibly indirectly against David, too, for not having removed his slippers when passing the mosque. A moment later, two or three shots from the beaters warned us that the boar had broken cover. A bullet whistled past me and broke a branch at my side, so I knew he was heading in my direction, but he swerved before I had sight of him and escaped. In spite of renewed activity from the beaters, this *battue* produced only very poor results— one jackal, that was all.

Now it was time to return to the clearing for our meal, but when we looked for the horses that should have been waiting to take us there, all but three had disappeared. Our grooms had "borrowed" them for a steeplechase, and we had no idea where they had gone. There was nothing for it but to walk, and I will do M. Florat and Mr. Saint-Leger the justice to add that, though one was a Catholic and the other Protestant, they unanimously forgot their religious differences and both swore like pagans all the way back to the rendezvous.

There we lit a fire, for M. Florat had brought some beef to be sliced very thinly and cooked on the embers, and were unpacking the rest of our provisions (a ham, two or three roast chickens and a dozen bottles of wine) when we saw our horses and servants coming back at full gallop, the animals panting and covered with foam, the men breathless and exhausted. At sight of us the rascals were stupefied with amazement, slid down from their mounts and glided away like lizards into the undergrowth. Only two or three, less nimble than the rest, were caught by the owners of the horses.

Then there began one of those bastinados of the East, a punishment we have no conception of in France. Even to witness it revolts any Frenchman who has not spent long years on the far side of the Mediterranean. If this chastisement had been given by Arabs to Moors, or by Moors to Arabs, the bystanders would probably have shown little or no interest, considering it merely a family affair. But for Christians to thrash true believers was a very different matter, and under the hoods of burnooses dark eyes began to flash ominously. I mentioned this to the gentlemen concerned, but without avail, for they would not cut short their vengeance on the wretched grooms. The one who received most punishment was the poor devil of a Negro, who rolled howling on the ground long after the last blow had fallen. The one who groaned the loudest, after him, was a Jew. The Arabs endured their sufferings without a sound.

When at last the Negro stood up again, long after the others, he once more took charge of M. Florat's gun and wandered off to join the group of beaters, while we began our lunch. I advised my friends to keep their weapons within reach and not to lose sight of the Arabs, for I was unpleasantly impressed by their expressions of hatred and fury while the bastinado was taking place. I made the same comment to our companions from Tangier, but they gave less heed to my warning than I could have wished. However, we decided to command a view of the whole clearing by climbing upon the rocks, where some of us began carving chickens, others sliced ham or opened bottles, while Boulanger was busy with his sketchbook.

Around us in a circle sat the Arabs, their meal consisting of a few dates and a drink from the spring that from its source below the rocks flowed on in a shallow trickle for some fifty yards before the sun dried it up. For a moment my eyes rested on this tiny rivulet, like a green-fringed wrinkle on the desert's sandy face, then traveled on to the Negro, who had already completely forgotten his recent sufferings and was playing happily with M. Florat's gun as a monkey might have done, with none of the caution that marks a man familiar with firearms. Before I could point this out to M. Florat there was a lightning flash from the gun, and a bullet whistled over our heads to flatten itself against the rock on which we leaned. Instantly we were afoot, our weapons ready. Was it just a clumsy accident, or a deliberate attack? The Arabs also had started to their feet and seized their guns, while the whole clearing fell suddenly silent and still, except for the Negro, who was rolling on the ground, shrieking like a man in mortal agony. It seemed prudent to regard the affair as an accident, so M. Florat, watched in silence by the whole company, strode across to his servant, took the gun from him with one hand, and with the other gave him a taste of his hunting crop. Incidentally, it did not even break the skin, but the poor wretch yelled even louder than before.

Beyond any doubt, if the delinquent had been a Moor or an Arab, revolt would have broken out at once, but since he was only a Negro the matter could not even serve as a pretext, so the Arabs settled down again and we did likewise. The incident was over in a moment, but I just had time to notice a smile flickering on the lips of the Jews. For an instant, it had seemed that Arabs and Christians were about to fly at each others' throats.

38

Five minutes later, peace reigned again and the whole affair had been forgotten, except by my friends and myself. Possibly we had exaggerated its importance, but it threw a chill over the rest of our day's sport, and any Arab bullets that came in our direction, possibly quite innocently, as they had that morning, seemed fired with hostile intentions. Nevertheless the day passed without any untoward incident, except that once we had to cross a wood that had recently caught fire. Every tree, every bush, every tiny twig was black as charcoal, and when at last we emerged there was little to choose, in appearance, between us and the Negro.

In the final *battue*, at about five o'clock, a young boar was shot by a Moor, and then we were confronted by an unforeseen difficulty. While hunting, we had penetrated a few miles further into the forest, and Mr. Saint-Leger had ordered the *sais* to bring our horses to a certain spot to save us the fatigue of returning on foot, but we found the rendezvous completely deserted. Shouts and gunshots failed to evoke the slightest response. We should have to walk back to the clearing—which did not trouble us unduly, but to our dismay we found that not one of the Arabs or Moors would help carry the boar. To them it was "unclean," and the least touch would mean "defilement." No promises, no threats could induce them to change their minds. Even the Moor who had shot the beast shrank from it with the utmost horror!

You could never guess, Madame, who finally volunteered for this fatigue duty! It was Paul, whose laziness during our Spanish tour has become proverbial! He may have been born an Ishmaelite, but he certainly loves boar meat, and he managed to gain an ally in the person of Mr. Hay's cook, who had been sent to take charge of our food supplies. Our two porters began to look around for a branch strong enough to take a boar's weight, and needing therefore to be at least three inches thick. Branches of that size are rare in the forests of Morocco, and we could find nothing strong enough to serve our purpose. Fortunately, Providence, who so often came to our aid in Spain, appeared at this moment in the shape of an Arab

39

wood-cutter carrying over his shoulder just the sort of pole we wanted. But this time Providence seemed to have turned Mohammedan and to have acquired a superstitious horror of pork. We could not buy the pole no matter what we offered! Eventually, Paul and Mr. Hay's cook took it by force. I gave the wood-cutter thirty sous to console him a little. In France such a sum would have consoled him completely and at once, but not here! He scowled fiercely and followed us for a long time, making faces. I'm very much afraid, Madame, that from this moment, Providence will show us no more favors!

Paul and the cook tied the animal's feet together, passed the pole between his legs, settled the pole on their shoulders and staggered off, the rest of us following, or, rather, soon going on ahead. Since our *sais* had given us a second edition of their morning's misdeeds, we promised ourselves to give them a second edition of their punishment, revised and enlarged.

We had trudged on three or four miles in the direction of Tangier, and night had almost fallen, when suddenly, in the last glimmer of twilight, we saw a dozen horsemen surging toward us in the distance, looming larger, silhouetted for a moment on the crest of a hill, then rushing down on us like an avalanche. Our servants had returned! Whence? We never knew! Never have I seen or imagined such a whirlwind of demons unleashed on earth! Bronzed faces gleaming and disappearing in the gloom; white burnooses floating out like shrouds; the hollow, muffled hoof beats of galloping horses, almost invisible yet sweeping down on us as swiftly as a thunderbolt—all these gave to this race-by-night the semblance of a fantastic dream. As for me, I could have forgiven their faults in gratitude for the unexpected, entrancing thrill of their reappearance!

At ten paces from us they halted, slipped to the ground and instantly disappeared out of our reach, a precaution I considered extremely prudent on their part, to judge from the threats I had heard expressed all around me for the past half-hour! Paul and the cook were particularly glad to see them, for practical rather than poetic reasons. The boar was loaded on to Paul's horse, the rest of us settled ourselves in the saddle, though our mounts were excited and wild, and so we arrived in Tangier at ten o'clock in the evening. (It was on this occasion that we saw the crowds thronging round the fountain, intoxicated with fresh water and their own high spirits.)

We found David waiting for us with an invitation to attend a Jewish wedding celebration on the morrow. It would give us a unique opportunity of observing their traditional rites for such an occasion, and he himself would entertain us to lunch and dinner. So, with our plans already made for the next day, we returned to our beds, welcomed by a signal lantern hoisted on the mainmast of the *Véloce*.

5

A JEWISH WEDDING[1]

It was midday when we arrived at David's house, and lunch was served immediately. Never have I seen a table more scrupulously appointed, or been offered more appetizing fare. There was fresh butter of a quality I had not tasted since leaving France, perfect dates, superb figs, mutton cutlets, and fish delicately fried. The wine, made from David's own recipe, owed little or nothing to the grape, but was nevertheless excellent. I fancy that it was the liqueur known in the Middle Ages as hydromel.[2]

After our meal, David invited us to follow him to the bride's home, where the celebrations had already been going on for six days. This was the seventh, "the Day of Hennah," the most interesting part of the ceremony, when the bride would be conducted to her new home. A hundred yards from the house we could hear tambourines rattling, the scraping of violins and the tinkling of little bells, the characteristic music of Morocco with its strange, barbaric harmony. Curious sightseers were crowding around the door, but on seeing David they fell back and made way for us. We went through into a square courtyard surrounded by houses, each with its own balcony or roof garden overlooking the court. In the

1. The ceremonies which Dumas describes here are not typically Jewish as he suggests. Very similar rites are still practiced in Moorish communities.—*Ed.*
2. Known in England as mead.—*Ed.*

center grew an enormous fig tree, its every branch densely packed at the moment with Moorish and Jewish children. On two sides of the courtyard were benches for spectators, and here we were offered seats. A third side, giving on to the street, was occupied by three musicians, one playing a violin which he held before him like a cello, and two others beating Basque drums. The fourth side, the façade of the bride's home, was thronged by a dozen Jewish matrons arrayed in their richest robes, while through the doorway we glimpsed fifteen or twenty other women guests.

All the surrounding roof tops were crowded, mostly with squatting Moorish women, ghostly shapes swathed in great blue or white blankets called *abroks*. Now and again, one would rise, give a kind of long drawn-out laugh like the gobbling of a turkey or the shriek of some great sea bird, then settle down again into her former immobility. Among them there was one who ran lightly from one balcony to the next, leaping the gaps between them with an agility lovely to behold, and giving us an occasional glimpse of her charming head in defiance of all the laws of the Prophet, letting her *abrok* slip to her shoulders for a moment, then raising it again with the laugh of a born coquette.

For some little time we sat absorbing the color and harmony of the scene, watching the children in the fig tree, the frenzied musicians, the statuesque groups of Jewish wives, the Moorish women on their balconies or house tops. Then, to provide us with further entertainment, David spoke to one of the women of the bride's family, who blushed deeply but came forward without further persuasion. Before the door was an empty space covered by a carpet, and in the center of this square she began to dance. The dances of Spain, the fandango, the cachucha, the *olé*, the *jaleo* had spoiled us, and anything less exuberant gave us little pleasure. Jewish dancing is not really a dance at all, just a series of steps on the same spot, with a hip movement reminiscent of the Andalusian *menito*. Little grace, except in the hands holding the customary kerchief twisted like a rope; no voluptuousness, except in the eyes; no originality or variation in skill to be discerned in any of the ten or twelve women who danced for us in turn to the accompaniment of the same plaintive air. It was scarcely a tune at all, just a monotonous cadence within the compass of a single octave, the rhythm marked by the older drummer, who laid aside his instrument and clapped his dry, fleshless hands together with a sound as of hollow wooden shells. To this accompaniment all the company sang a doleful refrain. Its subject? Madame, you would never guess! There are two historical events that will never be forgotten in Morocco, the bombardment of Tangier and the battle of Isly. The latter, as far as I know, has not yet been honored by a song, but the bombardment of Tangier is commemorated in a mournful ballad known to everyone, though why it should be sung as a dance tune at a Jewish wedding is a mystery I cannot explain.

The dance and the song were both cut off abruptly when David, who was obviously held in great respect by the whole Jewish community, invited us to go with him to see the bride in the crowded room that faced us across the courtyard. She had been lying on a great bed, surrounded by four young girls who seemed to be guarding her, but now she was made to rise and walk across the room to sit with her back against a wall. A scarlet veil covered her head and her eyes were fast closed. Indeed, she had not opened them since the ceremonies began a week ago.

On the first day, which was the Wednesday before our arrival, the musicians had begun their performance in the courtyard, while within the house the bride submitted to the ministrations of her family. First they bathed her from head to foot, then placed her on the bed where she would remain until the seventh day, and finally closed her eyes, forbidding her to open them until her gaze could rest on her husband's face. On Thursday, the bride's relatives ran through the town, inviting all her friends to come to her home on Saturday; Friday was spent preparing the feast for the next day, and on Saturday, at six in the morning, the young girls whom the bride had invited began to arrive and join her on the bed

44

where she still lay. At nine or ten o'clock the groom and his friends, after a service in the synagogue, arrived at the house to spend the day in feasting, but the bride herself was not allowed to open her eyes or rise from the bed. All night long the musicians played and the guests continued their festivities; on Sunday the house was cleansed and set in order, and on Sunday evening the bride sent gifts to her bridegroom— mattresses, bed coverings, clothing—which were escorted through the streets by the women of the family chanting: "*Hulahleh!* Hallelujah!"

From early morning on Monday the household was busy preparing a feast for the women, and when the banquet was over the bride was taken to the ceremonial baths at the synagogue. Tuesday, the Day of Hennah, began with dancing and singing such as we had seen on our arrival, but at noon it was customary to begin the bride's toilet by staining her fingernails and toenails brick red with henna. It was this ceremony that David had brought us to see, and it took half an hour to complete. Then she was conducted back to her bed, amid the strident laughter of the watching Moorish women. There would be nothing more for us to see until six o'clock in the evening, when, decked in traditional finery, the bride would be taken to her new home, so we decided to spend our time elsewhere until then. As we passed through the courtyard we asked David to give a few duros on our behalf to the dancer performing at that moment, for it is customary for foreigners who are admitted to such celebrations to pay a tribute to those who have entertained them. Indeed, we were happy to do so, for the curious spectacle had given us a great deal of pleasure.

All afternoon we explored the streets of Tangier, then completed our purchases at David's house, where an excellent dinner was set before us at four o'clock. At six we made our way back to the bride's home, but found the nearby streets now so crowded by curious sightseers that without David's help I doubt whether we should have been able to pass. Scarcely had we seated ourselves at one end of the room, which was about twenty feet long and not more than eight feet wide, when red damask curtains at the far end were drawn back to reveal the bride surrounded by her maids. She was brought to the middle of the assembly and perched upon a raised chair, where the matrons surrounded her, removed her red veil and began to dress her hair. When that was arranged to their liking, they piled upon it three separate head-dresses, one above the other; then a sash twisted round like a stove pipe on which they finally placed a coronet of red velvet shaped into points like the ancient crown of the Frankish kings.

Then a woman with a fine brush began to paint her eyelids and eyebrows with kohl, while another came up to her with two pieces of gilded paper prepared with cochineal. In turn the attendant licked each of these, placed it, all damp, upon the bride's cheek, gave a few rubs which could certainly have been lighter and gentler, and by this simple process created a vivid carmine blush, while the poor victim never opened her eyes or made the slightest movement. Now she was led from her chair to a kind of throne placed upon a table, and there she sat, still as a Japanese statue, while her brother, candle in hand, displayed her to all the world, and the women of the family fanned her with their handkerchiefs. For half an hour we all waited in silence, hearing nothing except the raucous laughter of Moorish women every ten minutes or so, and an undulating thread of sound from the musicians in the courtyard.

Suddenly the music broke out with redoubled energy into a fierce, triumphant rhythm and torches appeared, borne aloft in the hands of the bridegroom's relatives, come to fetch home the bride. Her throne was lifted bodily from the table and set upon the floor, while everyone applauded. Now, all those not belonging to the family were sent away, ourselves last of all. Four janissaries, each with a lantern in one hand and a staff or cudgel in the other, were waiting at the outer gate to make a way through the crowd for the bridal procession, and also to protect us, should that prove necessary.

The procession began to move forward, led by the bride, her eyes still tightly shut, her every movement stiff and mechanical. Three men were guiding her, one at each side with a hand beneath her arm, the third walking behind her, holding up her head, while all the wedding guests followed. Facing the bride were three other men bearing torches and walking backward, pushing away the crowd of sightseers, who were therefore forced to walk backward also. The whole scene, therefore, was sharply divided into two distinct groups, the bride and wedding guests advancing, the curious onlookers retreating, while between them a blaze of light, like a great hearth, shone upon the strange faces and diverse costumes of Moors and Jews, Arabs and Christians. It flickered along the house walls, where every doorway was crowded with veiled women, and into narrow side turnings barred by tall black specters, invisible but for the winding sheets that showed their outlines. It reached even to the roof tops, where a crowd of dark shadows rushed along in mid-air, jumping from roof to roof in pursuit of this clamorous, shining procession that seemed to be pushing before it, or drawing in its wake, the whole population of Tangier. It was the most fantastic sight I have ever seen in my life. As long as I live I shall remember these groups of white phantoms and the Jewish women with their pearl headdresses and gold-encrusted bodices; these little square windows, each framing a protruding head; and, above all, these demons of the night, swirling along the roof tops in the fringe of the torchlight, stopping only when an intervening roadway made the gap between houses too wide for them to cross. Even then, some managed to leap soundlessly over the empty space, as though curiosity had endowed them with the silent wings of a bat.

On we went for about an hour. I was in the first rank of the backward-walking sightseers, immediately behind the torchbearers and with a janissary at each side who vigorously protected me not only from violence but even from the slightest contact with the crowd around me. When at last we arrived at the house the bridegroom was squatting against the outside wall, motionless and with downcast eyes, like a stone statue set to guard the door. He might have been twenty-two or twenty-four years old and was dressed in black, his head freshly shaved, a thin thread of beard running under his chin from ear to ear. Not the slightest flicker of interest crossed his face as the bridal group approached. My friends and I entered the house, still under the protection of the janissaries, and the bride followed us to the threshold. There she halted and a glass of water was offered to her. She drank it, the glass was at once broken, and she was led to a throne like the one she had used in her childhood home an hour or two ago. Laughter, conversation and music began again and lasted for some ten minutes, during which time neither the bride on her throne nor the bridegroom sitting by the wall gave the faintest sign of life. Then five or six matrons lifted the bride down, carried her across to her bed, drew the curtains round her, and shepherded all the guests away. I do not know whether the hapless girl had ever seen the house that was to be her home, or looked upon the man who was now her husband. If not, the poor child must have been disagreeably surprised when at last she opened her eyes, for the place was poverty-stricken and the man extremely ugly.

It was ten o'clock when we left, and the lights were all out, the crowds vanished, the streets empty except for one or two solitary figures gliding past the silent walls. All the noisy hum and gay profusion had vanished like a dream, and the little fountain itself was lonely and silent, but for the sound of water dripping gently on the stones. Ten minutes later we were outside the town and had said adieu to Tangier, which we were unlikely ever to see again.

On the quay, David was waiting to take leave of us. During the afternoon he had had all our purchases taken out to the *Véloce*, and had also sent a messenger bearing a letter from M. Florat to the Bey of Tetuan, advising him that we should arrive there in two days' time. We wished to settle with David for the excellent meals he had provided and the stores of tobacco and dates he had sent us, but he would not hear a word about payment, and begged us not to distress him by insisting. I wish the most honest Christians of my acquaintance had his courtesy, his consideration for others, and his integrity.

6

GIBRALTAR

We arrived on board the *Véloce* at half-past ten, sat at table over supper until midnight, and stayed on deck till one o'clock in the morning, so reluctant were we to lose sight of Tangier, town of fantasy, that had regaled us with so many strange sights.

We were due to sail at four o'clock and I asked to be wakened at that hour, for I was anxious not to miss a single detail of our passage to Gibraltar, a place which, despite the ravages of modern materialism, still retains some of the enchantment given to her by the poets of antiquity. My request was forgotten, but the motion of the ship roused me and at five I was on deck. It was still dark, though one could sense the approach of dawn. On my right lay the coast of Africa, the Montagne des Singes a mass of aquamarine outlined against the paler azure of the sky already warmed by the sun's first rays. On my left the southern tip of Spain still lay in darkness, with the lighthouse at Tarifa shining out to sea. We were steering toward the middle of the strait, and, in the half-light, two brilliant streams of phosphorescence thrown up by our paddle wheels trailed behind us to lose themselves in our wake.

Slowly the sky grew brighter, until we could make out the African coast as far as Ceuta, the mountain, now aquamarine against orange, looking like a gigantic camel lying on the shore and drinking from the sea, Ceuta forming its head. As dawn touched Spain we could clearly see its towns and villages, its isolated homesteads, its valleys and mountain ranges running down to the sea. The coast we were leaving was desolate in comparison—no little townships, no hamlets, not even a *douar*[1] or a *gourbi*.[2]

As the sun rose like a globe of fire over Ceuta, we could see Gibraltar distinctly, her fortresses white in the morning light, her harbor wrapped in a blanket of fog pierced by the masts and pennants of the ships lying there at anchor. We were now at the point where one sees to their best advantage those two mountains, Calpé and Abyla,[3] that face each other across the narrow strait. The ancients called them the Pillars of Hercules, and for centuries believed that beyond them lay nothing but darkness. When Hercules was young, the Mediterranean was a great land-locked basin, its western boundary a mountain chain. Hercules felt this arrangement required alteration, so, choosing a mountain with two crests, he braced his feet against one and his back against the other, forcing them apart till the granite was split to its foundations and the outer ocean came boiling through the gap. Even today these sundered crests seem ready to merge into one again.

Shall I tell you something, Madame, that will doubtless seem to you just as much a fable as this tale of Hercules? Gibraltar is the only place on the Spanish coast, indeed, in the whole of Spain, that has fog. Why should this be so? Without the slightest hesitation I reply: "Because Gibraltar belongs to England, and England is a foggy place!" Make no mistake, Madame, it is not Nature that creates fog, it is the English! Hercules once fought a great fight with Antaeus, the son of Earth, but the English go one better and challenge Mother Nature herself, and the best of it is they always seem

1. *Douar:* a group of Arab tents.—*Ed.*
2. *Gourbi:* an Arab hut, built of interlaced branches covered with clay.—*Ed.*
3. Gibraltar was known to the ancient Greeks as Alybe, and to the Romans as Calpé. On the African side, the Monte del Hacko, once known as Abyla, is the highest of the seven peaks of the Montagne des Singes, or Apes' Hill, mentioned by Dumas earlier in this chapter.—*Ed.*

to win! Whatever they fancy, they manage to do! They grow
dahlias that smell like carnations, cherries with no stones,
gooseberries with no pips. At present they are busy growing
cattle with no legs! Look at the Durham breed![4] Their legs
are so short that they have only one joint and their bellies
practically touch the ground. Soon even that joint will doubtless disappear, and to move they will have to roll. It is just the
same with fog. There was never any fog in Gibraltar before
the English took possession. They were accustomed to fogs
and found they missed them, so they made some. What with,
Madame? Why, with coal, of course! Now there is so much
that if ever you visit Gibraltar you will acknowledge that
what I have told you is the simple truth. Look down from
the mountain side and you will see the whole town drowned
in fog, as though a tidal wave had engulfed it.

In any case, I was not visiting Gibraltar out of any special
enthusiasm for the town itself, but out of a twofold sense
of duty, first as a traveler (for when people ask me if I saw
the place, how could I possibly answer "No"!), and secondly
as a father, for Gibraltar might give me one last chance of finding Alexandre again, after losing him in Seville and waiting
in vain for him at Cadiz. Giraud and Desbarolles had not
given us a very attractive account of the place. They had
visited it earlier, and sworn never to set foot in it again, but
what would you? Man proposes, and God disposes! In all
fairness I should tell you that on that occasion they had
wandered everywhere, busily sketching everything they saw,
and had been taken for French sappers, disguised as Spaniards,
making plans of the English fortifications.

Ever since the English took Gibraltar, it has been an anxiety
to them, a constant worry, an obsession. They have suf-

4. Dumas' remarks (not to be taken too literally!), refer to the breed-
ing experiments carried out at the end of the eighteenth century by
the brothers Charles and Robert Colling, of Ketton, near Darlington,
with the purpose of improving the beef-making qualities of the cattle
in the Tees-water district of Durham. Their work had a great influence upon the development of shorthorn cattle, still called the Durham
breed in most parts of the world except this country.—*Ed.*

fered from this malady for almost a hundred years. For the first twenty-five it was acute, then it became chronic. At least once a week the First Lord of the Admiralty dreams that someone is capturing Gibraltar; he wakes in a fever of apprehension, summons his secretary, dictates a dispatch, and sends a man-o'-war with orders to the Governor to build a new fort, or raise a new rampart, or construct a new defense post, and, above all, to install more cannon. Already there are three thousand, and a standing reward of £2,000, that is 50,000 francs, is on offer to anyone who can suggest a spot in Gibraltar where a new gun would be, not merely necessary, but of any conceivable use.

Imagine, then, how Giraud and Desbarolles were received in the midst of all this heavy artillery! First, an English soldier was detailed to follow them everywhere they went, as though one of them were Napoleon and the other Buonaparte and Gibraltar were a second Saint Helena; then they were officially advised not to walk in the town after eight o'clock at night; and finally they were ordered to leave before six the next morning. Their departure was watched through a telescope all across the Bay of Algeciras, then on the road from Algeciras to Tarifa, for as long as they and the road were visible. Then a vessel of four hundred horsepower was dispatched in haste to London to inform the First Lord of the Admiralty that Gibraltar had almost been captured by two French engineers, but the attack had fortunately not succeeded. The bank rate fluctuated wildly, but finally settled at par, whereupon London was reassured. Now, what would the authorities think when they saw Giraud and Desbarolles returning to Gibraltar two months later, this time aboard a French corvette? It was enough to send us all to the hulks or Botany Bay!

Whatever the risk, we dropped anchor at seven o'clock in the morning, just over a mile off shore. My first glance circled the harbor of Gibraltar, my second the port of Algeciras, hoping to see a steamship that might have brought Alexandre, but there was none. My last remaining hope was that he might have traveled down on the *Tage*, which plies between Lisbon and Valencia, calling at Cadiz, Gibraltar and Malaga. However, I could not go ashore to look for him yet. We had to wait for a visit from the Health Authority, a body composed of ill-looking men who ask where you have come from and take your passport with a pair of tongs, all the time holding their handkerchiefs over their noses. The only thing that disturbs the Health Authority is illness, especially infectious diseases that are rampant in India and spread westward through Cairo, Tunis and Tangier. Having come straight from Tangier we were especially suspect, but this did not in any way deter a score of little boats from surrounding the *Véloce*, ready to take us ashore as soon as the Health Authority declared us free of plague or cholera.

While waiting, I commissioned the owner of one of these boats to put back to shore and run to inquire at every inn whether young M. Alexandre Dumas had arrived. I promised him a good reward if he were successful, though not lavish enough to risk his foisting on me a spurious Alexandre. Having taken these measures, we sat down to a meal while waiting for the Health Authority, so that we need not spend time over lunch later. We were counting on leaving Gibraltar the same evening, not later than five o'clock, otherwise we should have to stay till the next morning. In spite of what Giraud and Desbarolles had told us, we persisted in thinking there must be more to see in the town than cannons and kilted Scotsmen. We had already seen a corps of Highlanders on the jetty, looking most picturesque, but, like cannon, when you have seen one you have seen them all, unless, of course, you happen to catch sight of one in an unexpected position.

We had just gone down to the Captain's quarters when Vial came running down after us and appeared in the doorway.

"Well! I see they've managed to hook him for you!"

"Whom?"

"Why, your son, of course! He's coming out now, and I saw him with my glass. A great fair-haired fellow."

We shot up on deck. Yes, it really was Alexandre, coming

54

out in the boat I had sent to find him, and waving vigorously the moment he caught sight of us. A heavy weight was lifted from my breast. I had not discussed my anxieties with my friends, but I had been seriously worried. He had been missing for a fortnight, and such scraps of news as I had gleaned were all disquieting. As he drew up alongside I was waiting on the lowest rung of the ladder and he threw his arms around my neck, laughing like a great, untidy child.

"My word," he cried. "If you had been a day later you would have found me dead of boredom!"

"Is Gibraltar as bad as that?"

"It's simply frightful!"

"Out of the mouths of babes," murmured Giraud as we climbed back up on deck, after I had gladly thrown to the boatman twice as much as I had promised him.

Do you insist, Madame, on knowing what happened to Alexandre during his fortnight? Then I will send you the long poem[5] he wrote during the forty-eight hours he was waiting for us to arrive. If it does not give you the whole story, your fruitful imagination will readily fill in the blanks. In brief, it tells of his romantic love affair with a beautiful Spanish maid whom he glimpsed on one of those magic balconies I told you of in my earlier letters. She listened to his serenades, returned him smile for smile and sigh for sigh, slipped her tiny hand through the lattice to receive his burning kisses, even vouchsafed him a brief, stolen meeting, but her jealous family forced them to part forever, each mourning a broken dream.

I can assure you of one thing, Madame. Alexandre came back to me with such an appetite that he ate at least half the food served for eight of us. Writing poetry must be extremely exhausting! As we rose from table the Health Authority came on board, recognized that it had no occasion to interfere with our plans, and gave us permission to go ashore. Ten minutes later we stepped on to the jetty. While waiting we had scanned the port through a telescope and had been most intrigued to

5. Dumas gives the whole poem of thirty-seven stanzas in the original text.—*Ed.*

watch a detachment of Highlanders guarding a post a little to our left. For most of us, the Scottish soldier, with his costume so far behind, or so far in advance of, the rest of civilization, exists only in the novels of Sir Walter Scott. Now, suddenly, at the other end of Europe, we found ourselves face to face with him as an incredible reality.

Turning to look at Gibraltar itself, I could well understand why the ancients made it one of the Pillars of Hercules. It would be difficult to conceive a more convincing explanation for this monolith towering fifteen hundred feet above us and apparently bearing no relation to the land around it. At first sight it looks like a Sphinx crouching at the water's edge, her hindquarters resting in Europe, her head gazing over the sea to Africa, and her forepaws stretching in front of her to form the most southerly point of our continent. All the rough places one sees on her hide, the warts on her paws, the pimples that, like Cicero, she has on her nose, are houses, forts, battlements, and the ants that swarm up and down and all around her—those are men.

When going ashore I had proposed taking my gun with me as usual, but I was quickly warned that no armed foreigner would be allowed to land on Gibraltar. I was even forbidden to fire at a seagull in the harbor, and I humbly bowed my head in obedience to both injunctions. As we came in to land, we could see a new line of fortifications being hollowed out from the bed of the sea itself. I threw one last glance toward Algeciras on the far side of the bay, and saw it shining like a great fish with its silvery back half out of the water. I had a firm impression that on entering Gibraltar I was leaving Spain and crossing a frontier into England. Indeed, Tangier, which we had just left, seemed much more Spanish than Gibraltar. Here were none of those sharp-pointed cobblestones we had grown to know so well, no houses with green shutters or iron latticework to their windows, none of those charming patios with marble fountains. Instead, drapers' shops, cutlers, gunsmiths and hotels displayed over their doors the British coat of arms, while the pavements were thronged with fair-haired women and blond, rosy-cheeked officers. We went into a restaurant where they served us rare beefsteaks, sandwiches and butter, and when we called for a glass of malaga after our meal, the proprietor had to send out for it. He did, however, give us a perfect cup of tea—the finest pekoe.

We had asked permission to pay our respects to the Governor, but he had gone riding, so while awaiting his return we explored Gibraltar. In some of the side streets we found ourselves transported in a flash from England to Spain, or Africa, or Judea, for natives of those countries form a substantial proportion of the population, but, like most French visitors, we were chiefly concerned to see the monkeys. They are not in a cage, as mine are at home, or in a house of their own like the pets of M. de Rothschild, or in a palace such as we find in the *Jardin des Plantes*. They are completely free, chasing each other up and down the mountain, leaping from tree to tree, sometimes somersaulting down into the town itself. In fact, Gibraltar is the only place in our continent where monkeys have made themselves at home. Like the Arabs, they crossed from Abyla to Calpé, but, more prudent than humans, they did not venture forth into Spain or France, and so did not encounter a Charles Martel or a Ferdinand. In consequence, they have retained their conquest. They have done more, and, besides being entertaining, they perform a very useful function.

The English brought barometers to Gibraltar, but in the midst of all that fog the poor instruments were thrown completely out of gear. Bewildered by the constant struggle between mist and sunshine, they dared not venture to indicate "set fair" or "stormy," but always pointed to "changeable," which means nothing at all. So the monkeys stepped into the breach and made themselves barometers. Calpé has two sides, one facing east, the other west. If the weather is "set fair," the monkeys play on the western slope; when storms and tempests threaten, they move to the eastern side. One can readily understand that once they had acquired this important habit, the monkeys of Gibraltar became as sacred as grasshoppers in Holland or the ibis in Egypt, and very serious penalties are imposed upon any person killing one.

The weather was "set fair," so we explored a charming walk on the western slope, hoping we might get a close view of a macaque or a Barbary ape, but, alas, they eluded us. What I did observe, however, was the most curious combination of earth, trees and flowers to be found anywhere in the world, for the flowers came from England, the trees from France, and the soil was brought here from Heaven knows where, a few handfuls at a time, in wheelbarrows, on the back of a mule, or in a ship's hold. Unfortunately, these attempts to create a garden have been handicapped by the military development of the place, and the whole mountain side is bristling with guns and stiff with sentries. Beyond lies the ever moving, limpid blue sea that no human power can change. If that were not so, it would doubtless by now have become as gray and choppy as the Straits of Dover.

We caught sight of three horsemen riding down one of the mountain slopes—the Governor and two of his aides, as we were told—so we said a regretful good-by to the monkeys we had scarcely seen, and thankfully left the guns and sentries of which we had seen too much, and made our way toward Government House. Perhaps you are surprised, Madame, that I was so set on visiting any governor, especially the Governor of Gibraltar, but I have forgotten to tell you that his name was Sir Robert Wilson. You, Madame, are too young to recall this name, which Frenchmen of my generation will always hold in veneration because of an event which took place in 1815.

The disaster of Waterloo was still reverberating over Europe like a gigantic landslide; the *Northumberland* had just left England, bearing to Saint Helena that bewildered genius who in a moment of folly had asked his bitterest enemies for shelter; Louis XVIII, after an absence of three months, had re-entered the Tuileries, in his hand a list of "traitors" condemned to death. On this list the names of three men stood out in red as though written in blood: La Bédoyère, sentenced

58

by court-martial; Ney, condemned by the Chamber of Peers; and Lavalette, whom a jury found guilty of treason. La Bédoyère and Ney were both executed, the shots of their firing parties re-echoing over Paris. Lavalette alone remained. There had been some hope that the jury would acquit him, or, if they found him guilty, would recommend mercy, but both prophecies proved false. The 21st, 22nd and 23rd of September, 1815, were terrible days for all Paris. The Court of Cassation rejected his appeal on the 20th, which meant execution in three days. This time it would not be by firing squad, that soldierly death which carries no shame, for the victim faces his executioners and is still in command. This time it would be the shameful death of a public execution at the hands of the official butchers, with all the hideous panoply of the guillotine. Lavalette, as a former aide-de-camp of Buonaparte himself, had petitioned to be allowed to face a firing squad, but Louis considered this favor too great and had refused.

The bloody event was due to take place on the morning of the 24th, and in the first light of dawn crowds began to throng every bridge, quay and open space near the place of execution, for the guillotine has her devotees, and whether the head that falls be innocent or guilty, the drama is the same. However, this time the sullen crowd waited in silence, half curious, half in fear. Suddenly a strange, unexpected rumor ran through the waiting throng, and joyous cheers broke out. When the executioner entered the condemned cell to bring out his victim, he found no one there except a woman, Madame Lavalette. The evening before, she and her daughter had come to sup with the condemned man whom they planned to save, and at eight o'clock M. de Lavalette, dressed in his wife's clothes, had walked out of the *Conciergerie* on his daughter's arm to a sedan chair in which they were both carried away by the usual porters, who were not in the plot. They gave evidence that on the Quai des Orfèvres, near a little side street, a man stopped the chair, drew aside the curtain and said to the taller of the two ladies:

"Madame, you still have to call on the President." The smaller lady remained in the sedan chair while the taller took the arm of the gentleman who had spoken to her and walked with him into the side street. A moment later, the porters heard a carriage being driven away at full gallop. Nothing else was known, except that M. de Lavalette had certainly not passed through the gates of Paris and his recapture was expected at any moment. But day after day went by without news, until three and a half months had passed, and then at last, on January 15, the rumor ran that Lavalette had not only managed to leave Paris but was safely out of France. No one believed the story at first, for the details seemed incredible. M. de Lavalette had passed through the gates at eight o'clock one morning, in an open carriage driven by an English colonel, who had taken him right across France and had not left his side until they reached Mons, over the frontier and into Belgium, where Lavalette was in perfect safety. This Englishman was Sir Robert Wilson, now Governor of Gibraltar, and you can appreciate why I longed to meet him.

Sir Robert, a grand old man of sixty-six or sixty-eight years, who still walks twenty miles a day around Gibraltar, received me in charming fashion. I rashly showed an interest in his collection of Moroccan pottery, and when I returned to the *Véloce* it was waiting there for me. If anything could have persuaded me to spend another day in Gibraltar, Sir Robert's pressing invitation for the morrow would have done so, for I felt a glow of admiration for this noble, loyal-hearted man. May God give him long and happy days, for another man owed him the same boon.

We left the quay just in time. Ten minutes later and we should have had to stay in the town till morning. As we climbed aboard the *Véloce* we drew a deep breath of relief, just as M. de Lavalette must have done when he set foot on the cobblestones of the Quai des Orfèvres.

7

❧　❧　❧

THE RESCUE OF CERTAIN
FRENCH PRISONERS

We weighed anchor at four o'clock in the morning of November 26 and steered diagonally across the Strait on a line forming an acute angle with our course of the day before, Gibraltar being at the apex. At nine we found ourselves in an immense bay where, on our right, the mountains of Cape Negro swept down to form a valley with Tetuán lying at the bottom of the hollow and looking more like a great racecourse than a town.

During the crossing I had a long chat with the Captain, who gave me some very interesting information. In order to fetch me from Cadiz without delay, the *Véloce* had been diverted from a commission on which she was already engaged, namely, the rescue of certain French prisoners now in the hands of Abd-el-Kader. This was the first I had heard of any such mission and I begged the Captain to tell me every detail. I was especially anxious to know whether there was still time to carry out the original plan, and he told me exactly how matters stood.

You will remember the heroic struggle at Sidi-Ibrahim, the grief and shock it brought to every French heart. After that battle, the Arabs took some five hundred of our men prisoner, the most notable among them being M. Courby de Cognord, who commanded a squadron of hussars. The massacre at Mouzaia, so vividly reported by Roland, the trumpeter who witnessed it and managed to escape only by a miracle, reduced the number of prisoners to twelve. Any hope of ever seeing these men again had been given up when, on the fifth of October last, M. Courby de Cognord wrote to the Governor of Melilla a letter that reached him on the tenth of the same month. This letter informed the Governor that M. de Cognord had just succeeded in coming to terms with his Arab guards, who had agreed to assist him and the other prisoners to escape, for a reward of 6,000 doros which Courby de Cognord begged the Governor to lend him on his personal promise of repayment.

The Governor of Melilla was unable to raise such a sum himself, so he at once passed de Cognord's letter to the French consul at Malaga, who referred it to the Governor of Oran. When writing to the French consul, the Governor of Melilla also sent to M. de Cognord a letter dated October 17, regretting his inability to provide the money himself and explaining what steps he had taken to ensure that it would be made available.

The moment the Governor of Oran received the dispatch from the French consul at Malaga, he sent for the captain of the *Véloce*, asking him to bring one of his officers with him. The Captain immediately obeyed, taking with him his first sub-lieutenant, M. Durande. The outcome of this interview was that Commandant Bérard was ordered to go instantly to Melilla with M. Durande, to confer with the governor of that fortress upon the best means of bringing negotiations to a satisfactory conclusion. At the same time, the Treasury at Oran handed Bérard the sum of 32,000 francs named as the promised reward, plus a further 1,000 francs for unforeseen expenses, though the written instructions given to him at the same time made it plain that the authorities entertained little hope for the prisoners. While he was free to act as he thought fit, he was warned to be cautious and on his guard against treachery. He was to land M. Durande at Melilla, "if it proved possible to do so without risking his being robbed," but if there was the slightest cause for suspicion he was to return to Oran immediately, bringing M. Durande and the money with him. To avoid rousing any curiosity—Arabs being by nature extremely suspicious—the *Véloce* would put in at Melilla simply to land M. Durande "for reasons of health." If he found it expedient to stay ashore, well and good; if not, he must at once return to the ship, which, in either event, was to leave Melilla with the least possible delay.

As it turned out, M. Durande came back at once, for the Governor refused to allow him to remain without written authority from the Governor-General of Granada. However, the Governor was satisfied that the proposed negotiation could be taken seriously, and when Commandant Bérard explained what M. Durande's orders were, the Governor agreed to co-operate, placed the money in safe keeping and issued an official receipt. On the same day, the Governor of Melilla sent a special messenger, one of his own Arab interpreters, to M. de Cognord with a letter informing him that the ransom was already in the Governor's hands.

This emissary presented himself at the prisoners' quarters in the guise of a sick man who wished to consult the French doctor, a fine young man named Cabasse, who habitually ignored his own sufferings to attend to those of others. So the Governor's messenger, groaning and scarcely able to drag himself along the ground, was allowed to approach the prisoners, who had not the least idea that he was not what he seemed until the moment when, as Dr. Cabasse was feeling his pulse, he slipped the Governor's note into his hand. Instantly it was conveyed to M. de Cognord, who wrote in reply: "Your letter has given us great joy. Keep the money by you. We hope to be in your town shortly and to have an opportunity of expressing our gratitude." This message, in De Cognord's handwriting but unsigned, was passed to the Arab as though it contained a dose of medicine, and reached the Governor safely.

Meanwhile, the Arab chief who had arranged the plan of escape with M. de Cognord sent an emissary of his own, on November 6, to the chief of the Beni-Bouillafars, a neigh-

boring tribe who would help in the escape and share the reward. This chief, in his turn, sent a letter next day to the
Governor of Melilla, advising him that the prisoners could
be brought in either on the 23rd or the 27th, since those
were the days when his tribe would be in charge of the
observation lines outside the town. (The tribes around Melilla undertake this duty in rotation, every fourth day.)

To avoid giving the Arabs any grounds for suspicion, Commandant Bérard's instructions were that the *Véloce* was to
keep away from Melilla till the last possible moment. (This
explains why, in order to use his waiting time to the best
advantage, he had been sent to pick me up at Cadiz.) However, to ensure that help and a means of transport should be
immediately available for the prisoners, M. Durande was ordered to sail up and down between Melilla and Djema-r'
Azouat in a felucca flying the Spanish flag. All this the Captain explained to me as we crossed from Gibraltar to Tetuán.

It was now the 26th, the very day when the prisoners'
fate hung in the balance. My first impulse was to renounce
all thought of visiting Tetuán and to press on without delay, but the Commandant advised that since the Arabs were
unlikely to fulfill any promise till the last moment, it would
be wiser if the *Véloce* did not appear off Melilla before the
afternoon of the 27th, the later of the two dates suggested
by the chief of the Bouillafars. Accordingly, in spite of our
new preoccupations, we dropped anchor off Tetuán. Besides,
as I mentioned earlier, word had already been sent overland
from Tangier to inform the Bey of Tetuán that we would
visit his town, and since the arrangement had been made it
would be difficult to break our promise.

Accordingly we made ready to go ashore after lunch, but
scarcely had we sat down to table when the officer of the
watch informed us that two horsemen, apparently from Tetuán, were signaling to us from the shore. We went up on
deck and watched the riders cantering up and down, waving
their guns to attract our attention. They were richly dressed,
as we could see with the aid of the Captain's telescope, and

a boat was immediately ordered to go ashore to discover what they wanted. While waiting, we went down to finish our lunch so as to be ready for any eventuality, but curiosity brought us back on deck even before the boat touched the beach. We watched our sailors parleying with the Arabs, helped by a quartermaster who spoke Spanish, and after a short interchange the Arabs wheeled their horses and galloped off toward Tetuán, while the boat pulled back to the *Véloce*.

The horsemen were indeed emissaries of the Bey of Tetuán, come to confirm that we had actually arrived. Now they had gone back to fetch horses for us and to arrange an escort in our honor. We, however, were too impatient to wait till the promised escort arrived, and decided to take our guns and go ashore. Half an hour later we landed and spread out along the beach till we came to the mouth of a little river and explored its banks, bringing down a few marsh fowl. Then, since our escort was still not in sight, we made up our minds to walk toward the little town that we could see shining four or five miles away.

We were prevented by an unexpected obstacle. Five yards from the river bank stood a building we had taken for a farmhouse or a mill. It was, however, a combined guard post and customs office, and as we approached, soldiers of a sort came out, their gestures making it plain that we were not allowed to pass. Besides, they explained in bad Spanish, we had no need to proceed unaccompanied. If we would exercise our patience for just a few minutes, our escort would arrive.

We exercised our patience for an hour, an hour and a half —and were even more unlucky than Sister Anne, who did at last perceive two riders on the horizon while we saw nothing at all, so we decided to abandon any thought of visiting Tetuán and to return to the *Véloce*. The painters among us were heartbroken at first, for they had been promised marvelous subjects in the town, but I had only to give them a hint of what the Captain had told me about the prisoners.

At once a unanimous cry went up: "Back to the *Véloce!*" What to us was this little Arab town, even if it had been built in the days of Haroun-al-Raschid? It could not compare, at this moment, with the poor little Spanish fortress called Melilla.

So we were rowed out to our ship, and as the anchor was hauled up we saw, through the Captain's telescope, our promised escort just passing through the gates of Tetuán. An hour later we were scudding through the waves with our engines working at full pressure and with all sails set.

* * *

Melilla and Ceuta are the last footholds Spain has managed to retain in Africa. We will not occupy ourselves with Ceuta, for this ancient principality of Count Julian, the place whence the Moors bestrode the Straits of Gibraltar, has no importance for us save in its past. Melilla, on the other hand, has a burning interest for us in the present. It is Spain's Botany Bay, her convict settlement, and no corner of the world can hold more sadness for an exile.

He can almost see his native land on the horizon, yet knows he will never set foot on it again. There can be no escape from Melilla, as from other prisons, for should a man break away he will inevitably fall into Arab hands and lose his head. The Arabs have always been bitterly hostile toward Melilla and its garrison, except for an uneasy truce on market days. At other times the tribesmen creep to the foot of the ramparts to hurl stones, now and then to fire a shot or two. When the Governor takes offense and has the gates kept shut, the garrison has to eat salt beef. When the gates are reopened, the men of Melilla can enjoy fresh meat again at a price which includes the risk of theft or murder. The eight hundred men stationed here must remain always on the alert, or their throats will be cut as they sleep. They live in a state of siege that has lasted for three hundred years—even longer than the siege of Troy—a siege that is never relaxed, for, as I said just now, every Arab tribe of the neighborhood takes its turn of duty around Melilla. Remembering this you can well understand why the Governor of Oran took such careful precautions to safeguard the 32,000 francs sent by M. Durande, for General Cavaignac had already been robbed during a similar negotiation.

All day long we talked only of the prisoners, their chances, for we all feared that their plan of escape was more likely to fail than to succeed. Was it feasible for an Arab chief to circumvent the watchfulness of Abd-el-Kader and snatch from him twelve important prisoners out of the hundreds he held captive? Some of us thought the plan might have come from Abd-el-Kader himself, working through an intermediary. But was it likely that this tyrant would release twelve heads for 32,000 francs when he could have demanded three times as much? The whole affair had the atmosphere of mystery and tragic uncertainty that characterizes all dealings with men of the Arab race, whose hearts are full of trickery, whose moods can change in a flash. Might not the whole plan be devised to provide an excuse for massacring all the other French prisoners, on the pretext that they were caught trying to escape? Then again, it seemed incredible that we, who had come to Africa by the merest chance, might help to provide a happy ending for a drama whose opening acts were so somber. I could not believe it, yet, of us all, I was the only one to feel a ray of hope.

Meanwhile the African coast unrolled on our right like a tattered ribbon, and on our left the coast of Spain lay on the horizon, intangible as a cloud, till, at about four in the afternoon, it vanished altogether. As night fell, a strong gale blew up and seasickness claimed its usual victims. Maquet took refuge in his cabin, Giraud in his hammock, and when we looked in to see how they were, we found Vial lying beside Giraud. For all of us, sleep was slow in coming. A high sea was running and the very chairs and stools staggered about as though they were drunk.

We were due off Melilla early in the morning, and when we were called at seven the fortress was in sight. The first thing I noticed as I went on deck was that we were now flying the English flag as a precaution. We dropped anchor, and instantly everyone was on deck. Through the telescope we could clearly see two or three little ships moored in the harbor, but M. Durande's felucca was not among them. There was nothing to show whether matters had gone well or ill. Now and again we saw a sentinel on the ramparts and that was all.

The Captain was debating whether to send a boat ashore, all of us clamoring to go in her if he did, when we saw a man appear on the quay and step into a small craft which at once left the shore. A few minutes later we watched it making in our direction, flying the Spanish flag, and as it drew nearer we recognized the man as a Spanish officer, waving to us with his handkerchief. But "within sight" is not the same as "within earshot," and his signals could mean either "Go away!" or "Come in closer"; "All is lost" or "All's well!" A quarter of an hour passed in an agony of uncertainty. The shore was completely deserted; two or three fishing boats sailed lazily up and down, trailing their nets; only the little dinghy seemed akin to us in spirit, aware of some hope or fear in harmony with our own. Every heart beat high with apprehension, every eye devoured the tiny craft. No one thought of putting off to meet her. We all stood waiting, a prey to every emotion that suspense can bring.

The handkerchief was still waving wildly, and now we could see that the man who held it was young, not more than twenty-five. The telescope was no help, it was even an irritation, for though it brought his features nearer it could not bring his voice. Still, his expression seemed joyful, so did his gestures, and now, through the noise of wind and waves we began to catch the sound of his wild cry. He seemed to be shouting one word over and over again, but we could not hear what it was. Surely the very fact that he was shouting meant that he brought good news? Bad tidings could have waited till he came up with us. Not a sound could be heard aboard the *Véloce*, where every man stood motionless,

68

holding his breath and straining his ears. At last, in an instant when the wind dropped, we caught the word "Saved," and as we waited, hardly daring to believe, the same cry reached us once more, this time unmistakably. A delirium of joy swept over us, and as we cheered and clapped every breast swelled, every eye was bright with tears. When the young officer came alongside, the Captain, passengers and crew all rushed to welcome him aboard.

Unfortunately, all the French he knew was the one word he had learned by heart to shout to us across the water, so Desbarolles, our own interpreter, at once became a man of considerable importance. The messenger, Don Luis Cappa, an adjutant from the garrison, told us that the prisoners were now safe, and was able to add enough information to satisfy our curiosity. This is how things fell out. The men in the fortress, who had received no word from the Bouillafars since the communication indicating the 23rd or the 27th, had waited with an anxiety equal to our own when the first date passed uneventfully. Then, on the 25th, at about seven in the morning, two Arabs brought news that the prisoners were only a few miles away, and would be handed over, in exchange for the ransom, at Bastinga Point. As soon as the party reached that rendezvous they would light a great fire as a signal.

One of the Arabs was detained as a hostage, and the other sent back to report that his message had been well received. M. Durande was in the harbor aboard the felucca, and resolved not to wait for the promised signal but to anticipate it. His crew of six were armed to the teeth, the money was sent on board in six bags, Don Luis insisted on joining M. Durande to enjoy the fun, and the felucca cast off. For a while they sailed along the coast just out of cannon range, as though peacefully fishing, until they reached the point mentioned by the Arabs. There they lay to, but scarcely had their sails dropped when four or five horsemen appeared on the shore, waving to them. In response the felucca moved in closer, not within range of their guns but near enough for M. Durande to parley with the riders. The prisoners, said the Arabs, were now only a mile or two away. M. Durande's interpreter replied that the reward was ready and held up a bag in each hand. Instantly one of the riders wheeled and galloped off, returning three-quarters of an hour later with the rest of his band and a group of prisoners, all on horseback. One soldier had died of fever the night before, so there were eleven prisoners in all, ten men and a woman who had been captured with her little daughter at the gates of Oran, eight years earlier.

At the sight of this pitiful group the young Spanish officer could not restrain himself for joy. He jumped overboard, swam to land and flung his arms around M. de Cognord, a great imprudence, of course, for nothing was as yet settled. The Spaniards of Melilla are at war with the neighboring tribes, and if things went awry, as well they might, Don Luis would have remained a prisoner in Arab hands. M. de Cognord told him so, as soon as he had strained him to his breast. "In Heaven's name," he cried, "get back on board!" "Oh, no!" returned Don Luis, enthusiastic as a boy. "When I left Melilla I swore that I would bring you back or share your captivity," and he took his stand with the prisoners.

Fortunately the Arabs seemed to be acting in good faith, and as anxious to claim the reward as M. Durande was to take the prisoners into safe keeping. They sent one of their chiefs aboard to count the money, and when he was satisfied that the amount was exactly right he put back to shore with three bags and sent out half the captives; then the remaining bags were collected and the rest of the prisoners were free to rejoin their companions. All of them could scarcely believe that their escape was an accomplished fact till they found themselves among their fellow countrymen, in a boat commanded by a French officer, their hands clutching a good carbine. They had been prisoners of the Arabs for fourteen months and twenty days, and their names were: Lieutenant Colonel Courby de Cognord; Lieutenant Larrazée; sub-lieutenant Thomas; Doctor Cabasse; Lieutenant Marin of the 15th Light; Sergeant Major Barbut of the 2nd Hussars; Testard and Metz, both hussars; Trotté, cavalryman of the 8th battalion, and Michel of the 41st; and the woman, Therèse Gilles. They were all taken to Melilla, where they passed the night, and early the following morning the felucca set sail for D'jema-r'Azouat.

Here, then, are the facts exactly as they occurred, dictated to me by Don Luis Cappa, Desbarolles acting as my interpreter and a midshipman serving me as a writing desk.

8

CELEBRATIONS AT
D'JEMA-R'AZOUAT

The prisoners, understandably anxious to be gone from Melilla, decided not to wait for the *Véloce* and had sailed eighteen hours before we arrived. We grew alarmed for their safety, since the wind was against them and the felucca, only a light craft, could easily be wrecked or blown on the rocky coast. The Arabs, having made sure of the reward, might well give chase in some of their own boats to recapture the men they had freed, and though we knew the fugitives would fight to the death rather than be taken, this would be a sorry end to the long negotiations.

Commandant Bérard did not waste an instant. With full hearts and warm handclasps we quickly said good-by to Don Luis and watched him slip over the side, down to his little boat, as the order went to our engine room: Full speed ahead. Unfortunately, as I said before, the *Véloce* was not a fast ship. She would take twenty-eight or thirty hours to reach D'jema-r'Azouat, and was unlikely to overtake the felucca en route. There, however, M. Durande would certainly put in for a while and we ought to catch up with him. All our officers agreed that he was too good a sailor to expose his passengers to a longer crossing in such a frail boat.

The sea grew rougher every minute and the wind stronger. Darkness fell early, the night was overcast and stormy. A special watch was kept, but we saw no sign of any felucca, and at daybreak we were off Maluénas. Toward eleven we

2

rounded Tres Forcas, and skirted the coast near enough to be sure of seeing anything between us and land. We saw the mouth of the Mulwiya, which serves roughly as the eastern boundary of Morocco and runs parallel with the Isly. Then came Cape Melonia, where General Cavaignac trapped the Arab tribe of the Beni-Snanens, who had earlier betrayed Colonel Montagnac with a treacherous message and so caused the disaster of Sidi-Ibrahim, where whole regiments of our finest troops were butchered. At Cape Melonia, four or five thousand of the Beni-Snanens had their throats cut before being thrown into the sea, for our soldiers were mad for revenge and gave no quarter. General Cavaignac almost lost his prestige with the whole army because he saved the remnants of this wretched tribe. The bugler, Roland, the only man to escape from the slaughter at Mulwiya, was also at Cape Melonia. He took such terrible revenge that night that even he was satisfied, for he killed more than thirty Arabs with his own hands.

As we drew near D'jema-r'Azouat we caught sight of two feluccas, one almost scraping the rocks on its way into port, the other doing its best to get out, but both were merely fishing boats, as we saw with our glass. D'jema-r'Azouat itself began to unroll before our eyes, stretching out to the south of the mountains with its newly built, widely scattered houses and its camp, sheltered in a fold of the hills. Beyond those hills lie two famous battlegrounds, as memorable as Thermopylae and Marathon—Sidi-Ibrahim and Isly.

We dropped anchor a mile or so off shore, and noticed great activity in the port and along the sandy beach where horsemen were galloping in all directions. The streets of the new town were thronged, while the camp seemed quite deserted. Several fishing boats lay at anchor in the harbor, but M. Durande's felucca was not among them, and, contrary to our expectations, it seemed as though the prisoners had pushed on toward Oran. Scarcely had we settled in our anchorage when a boat set off from the quay, bringing out the harbor master. As soon as he was close enough to hear us we begged

73

for news, and rejoiced to learn that the ex-prisoners had indeed reached D'jema-r'Azouat safely, thus completing, after fourteen months, the circle of their Odyssey. What sufferings, dangers and hardships, what fears and hopes, those fourteen months had brought them! When the harbor master came alongside he told us that M. Durande himself had already left for Oran, and we could appreciate this brave young man's anxiety to announce personally to General d'Arboville the happy outcome of the drama in which he had played a principal role.

It was now about two o'clock in the afternoon, and there was no time to lose if we were to leave again that evening. The Commandant ordered his boat to be launched at once, but some of us, I among them, were in such haste that we jumped into the harbor master's boat and were soon plowing through rough seas toward the shore. The ship's boat quickly overtook and passed us, with Maquet hanging over the bows and Giraud aft, both of them in a deplorable condition, but as determined as the rest of us to meet the men we had come so far to find. The Commandant's boat got in five minutes before we did, and as I stepped ashore the first two faces I saw were those of my old friends Major Picaud and Colonel Trembley, who told us of the great rejoicing at the arrival of M. de Cognord's party, adding that a grand banquet was being prepared for them that same evening.

We walked on toward the town, crossing a wide open grassland filled with cattle captured in a recent raid. Clearly, the raiders had brought in not only the cattle but their fleas as well, for by the time we reached the town gates we were black to the knees with these pests. In the square we met Colonel Mac-Mahon, who invited us to the evening's banquet, an invitation we gladly accepted. Then we were escorted to the most luxurious of the barracks where we were to meet M. de Cognord and his companions, who had been advised of our arrival.

As at Melilla, our hearts were full to overflowing. How strange is the way a shared emotion can bind together men

74

of entirely different natures till they seem as one! Six of us stood waiting there, profoundly unlike each other in outlook and temperament, yet when we heard steps approaching, when the door opened, when M. de Cognord was announced, every arm was outstretched in greeting. We were more moved than M. de Cognord and his companions, who for two days had known nothing but sympathetic greetings, embraces, congratulations. To them, we were just one more group of compatriots come to rejoice over their deliverance. To us, they were heroes and martyrs.

I suggested that while waiting for the evening's festivities we might visit the tomb of Captain Géreaux, the hero of Sidi-Ibrahim, who brought the tattered remnants of his column to within half a league of D'jema-r'Azouat before he and the other survivors of four days of battle were surrounded and slain. The proposal met with universal approval, and instantly six or eight horses and a guide were at our service, while several officers begged to accompany us. The tomb was raised over the fallen where they lay, in the valley of Rizi, under a cluster of gigantic fig trees, and the road to it is charming, lying in a cleft between wooded mountains and shaded by fig trees as tall as our oaks in France, while a little river winds beside the path. All along the road we came upon advance posts and stacks of muskets, as though the enemy was still there, as, indeed, he is, invisible now, but all the more to be feared and apt to strike suddenly when least expected. All around D'jema-r'Azouat are the treacherous tribes of Beni-Snanen, Souhalia and Ouled-Rizi, false friends, two-faced, perfidious allies who fondle with one hand and strike with the other. In the deep grass beside the road we heard the lowing of cattle and the tinkling of sheep bells. Shepherds tending their flocks rose slowly as we approached, stood motionless to watch us pass, then sank down again out of sight. Such herdsmen as these, their guns always handy in a nearby clump of bushes, act as spies for the tribes who are at all times on the point of revolt. Should an overconfident soldier wander off alone into these pastures, the patriarchal shepherd's crook is instantly dropped for an assassin's knife.

The tomb, erected lovingly, stone by stone, by men of the garrison of D'jema-r'Azouat, has a simple but beautiful shape, as befits a soldier's last resting place. May it remain so! God forbid that any architect should ever attempt to replace it by some coldly classical mausoleum. For my friends and myself it was strangely moving to see De Cognord and his companions, the sole survivors of the tragic drama, standing by the grave of the fallen, linking the two ends of that heroic chain.

I have never known anything so pitiful, so soul stirring, as our return toward D'jema-r'Azouat, every man speaking of a friend he had lost in this campaign. At every step, one officer or another would pause and say to the man beside him: "It was just here that so and so fell." "Yes, I remember," the other would reply with a smile, "he was the best and bravest of us all." In their eyes the fallen are always the noblest. The courage, the strength of these voluntary exiles, who battle against fever, hardships, surprise attacks, summer heat and winter cold, so far away from home! With the utmost respect I shake such men by the hand, with incredulous amazement I see them smile. My God! My God! When I think how reluctantly France counts out, sou by sou, the price of bare necessities—better bread for her troops, a hospital for the wounded, I could wish the Motherland were more worthy of her sons!

*　　*　　*

My train of thought was broken off as we re-entered the camp and found two or three hundred people lined up to welcome us back. During our absence, preparations for the evening's festivities had made great strides and a barn had been transformed into a banqueting hall, its walls draped with the tricolor, its whole length wreathed and festooned with the laurel that grows so freely in Africa. No one is more ingenious than the French soldier when it comes to improvising decorations out of whatever lies to hand, and when we

76

took our places at six o'clock bright stars shone down from ceiling and walls. The whole place blazed with light reflected everywhere from mirrors, and it seemed as though some powerful genie had been at work. How else could you explain a feast for three hundred people suddenly materializing on this lonely stretch of sandy, desert shore? All the former captives were present, except one. He, poor devil, had been excluded because the rumor ran that he had surrendered to the enemy. In Africa a soldier may win a fight, be killed or captured, but to surrender is unthinkable. He was awaiting court-martial, and meanwhile he was shunned like a leper, left alone in a solitary cabin. No one would have been surprised if he had blown out his brains as the first sounds of cheering and revelry reached him across the quiet sand. Indeed, his former comrades had left a pair of loaded pistols within his reach, for they felt he had brought dishonor to the regiment. What must such stern judges think of the capitulation at Baylen and the surrender of Paris?

So, amid the universal rejoicing there was a note of tragedy as we sat down to table, where honors were divided between the prisoners and ourselves. Colonel Mac-Mahon had Colonel Courby de Cognord on his right and myself on his left, while opposite us sat Commandant Bérard and Colonel Trembley. Then came Maquet, Boulanger, Giraud, Desbarolles and Alexandre, each between two ex-prisoners, while at the foot of the table, with their interpreter, sat two envoys from Abd-el-Kader, their white burnooses knotted around their brows with a camel cord. The regimental band, out of sight behind the draperies, played martial music. Only once in a lifetime can a man have the luck to be present at such a function, and he could never describe it, for emotion would choke him.

In champagne we toasted the King of France, the princes, the prisoners rescued so unexpectedly, the glorious dead; and every toast was received with a salvo of artillery that brought howls of response from the jackals in the nearby mountains. After the toasts came the speeches, recalling feats performed by the very heroes that sat among us laughing, singing, raising their glasses to the ceiling. One man, out hunting with his double-barreled gun, killed three of a band of six Arabs who attacked him and took a fourth prisoner; another, captured with ten of his men by a force of twelve hundred tribesmen, managed to bring nine safely back to camp. I felt I was among the ancient heroes of Herodotus or Xenophon, or that one of Cooper's stirring romances had come to life before my eyes. After the speeches came singing, and, I confess, dancing as well, while all the time the envoys of Abd-el-Kader calmly watched us in silence with their great velvet eyes, doubtless thinking us completely mad.

At last we rose, for the time had come to say good-by. Horses were waiting to take us back to the shore, and almost all the officers, Mac-Mahon and Trembley among them, insisted on riding that far with us. We exchanged adieus with the rest of the guests, left them to their singing and dancing, climbed into our saddles and rode regretfully away. Conversation flowed freely as we went, of France and Africa, Austerlitz and Isly, Marengo and the Pyramids, till all at once dead silence fell. As my friends and I looked about us to discover the cause, our companions pointed to a little hut standing all alone, and whispered: "That's where he is." They never spoke the name of the soldier who had surrendered, or let him hear the sound of a human voice. The Spartans themselves were no crueler than this to the man who fled from Thermopylae.

Half an hour later we reached the sea, and with full hearts said good-by. The night was fine, the moon magnificent, and as our boats pulled slowly out from shore our friends lined the water's edge, watching the furrow of phosphorescence that marked our passage and now and then shouting one more adieu. So at last we reached the *Véloce*, which was ready to sail the moment we came on board. As the anchor was raised we joined our voices in one final cheer and the crowded beach replied. For some time longer we could hear bursts of laughter and snatches of regimental music, till they grew faint

78

and died away in the distance. Then nothing remained but the fires of D'jema-r'Azouat and their flickering reflection in the water. Finally these too vanished as we doubled the eastern promontory of the bay. So ended a wonderful day, the 27th of November, 1846.

9

❧ ❧ ❧

ALGIERS AND BIZERTA

We had decided not to put in at Oran but to press on with
all speed to convey the good news to Algiers, and all day on
the 28th we made good progress along the coast. Maquet,
who had almost split his head open on some beam or other,
stayed in bed, while Giraud, ill with his dread seasickness, lay
all day in Vial's cabin, so that our circle was reduced to Alexandre, Desbarolles, Boulanger and myself.

At nine o'clock in the morning of the 29th, the cry of
"Algiers!" brought us all on deck, even drawing Maquet and
Giraud from their beds, to see the magnificent view of the
town from the sea. The buildings begin at the water's edge
and climb the whole eastern slope of the mountain, its summit
crowned by the Emperor's Fort, leaning slightly toward the
left. French buildings have completely spoiled the Eastern
atmosphere that formerly characterized Algiers, so that now,
at first sight, it looks almost European. To find the ancient
town of the *deys* your eye must go beyond the foreground
and follow up the mountain side. Even there, in between the
old, low, white houses with their few narrow slits of windows,
you see new, square, four-story buildings like those at home in
the *faubourg* Saint Denis, with great wide windows to let in
all the sunshine. A few fine palm trees stand silhouetted against
the whitewashed walls or the azure sky, silently resisting this
French invasion. To our right, the sea lay open beyond
Majorca to Montpellier; to our left, the plain of Metija

80

stretched along the coast from Rassauta to Ben-Afroun; behind us rose Cape Matifu, with Atlas beyond.

We sailed past the jetty that seems the work of Titans but was built by human hands with blocks of concrete—the same jetty that the French government has been debating for the last ten years—and scarcely had we dropped anchor when a boat came rowing out to us to inquire for news. The result of the plan to rescue the prisoners was still unknown at Algiers, so our haste to bring information was fully warranted. Our story caused a great sensation among the army men. As for the shopkeepers, traders and speculators, they are the same on the far side of the Mediterranean as they are on this. Some of them even asked us what prisoners we were talking about!

We were disappointed to find that Marshal Bugeaud had left Algiers a few days earlier, and had gone overland to Oran with two or three *députés* who were visiting Algeria during their parliamentary recess. In his absence, General de Bar was in command of the town. Quickly we made fresh plans. Since Marshal Bugeaud would be away about a fortnight, and our recommendation was to him personally, I decided to turn these fifteen days to good account by going on to Tunis and returning via Bona, Philippeville and Constantine. Accordingly, taking with me the official letter placing the *Véloce* at my service, I called on General de Bar, who referred me to Rear Admiral de Rigodie.

I hope Mme de Rigodie will allow me to record my thanks for a delightful hour spent in her company while Commandant Bérard was receiving fresh orders from the Rear Admiral, who, as I hoped and expected, confirmed that the *Véloce* was to take me wherever I wished to go, but advised us to return to Algiers not later than December 20. As a special favor to me he sent an old friend of mine to join our party, Monsieur Ausone de Chancel, who is well known in France for his delightful poetry and in Algeria for his serious works.

This was the simple arrangement that was so hotly challenged in government circles and was called a "misunderstanding" by the *Ministre de la Marine* in that celebrated session in the Chamber when I was referred to as *"ce monsieur."* Alas! one of the men who were so quick to insult me has since died. The names of the other two I have forgotten. The fact that this vessel was placed at my service has made me more enemies than *Anthony* or *Monte-Cristo*, and that is saying a good deal.

But that is our way in France. We are irritated when anyone is shown a favor, wounded when an honor is accorded—except to ourselves. I think it was in 1823 or 1824[1] that Sir Walter Scott was ill and expressed his longing for a voyage to Italy. At once the Admiralty placed its finest frigate at the service of the author of *Ivanhoe* and all England, including both Houses of Parliament, applauded the gesture. It was an excellent idea, for in every Mediterranean port, perhaps for the first time in history, the English flag was welcomed with wild enthusiasm, out of regard for the man of genius whom it sheltered. True, I may justly be told that I am not Sir Walter Scott, but I would reply that France never recognizes her sons for what they are, while they are alive.

But the fact remains that the *Véloce*, either as a favor or my just deserts, was placed at my command for those three weeks, and the government put an extra tax on coal to pay for it! It is as well for the public to know that this voyage, which caused so much outcry, cost the country 16,000 francs, exactly half what it cost me personally.

So our first call at Algiers was merely a brief halt, and we counted on exploring the place later, on our return. I confess that it gave me keen pleasure to find myself back on the *Véloce* and on my way to visit Tunis, the town of Saint Louis, and Carthage, the home of Dido and Hannibal. For two days and nights we hugged the coast, until, at about 11

1. Dumas' impression of this date was inaccurate. It was in 1831 that Sir Walter Scott began his cruise in the Mediterranean which lasted for the greater part of a year and ended in the summer of 1832, when he was brought back to Scotland and died at Abbotsford in September.—*Ed*.

A.M. on the third day a charming little town appeared, quite Eastern this time, lying on the edge of a gulf whose waters were a wonderful blue—Bizerta. The very name is full of magic, and with one voice my friends asked: "Shall we be visiting Bizerta?"

"Would it be any trouble?" I asked Commandant Bérard.

"None at all," he replied, and an hour later we stepped ashore from the yawl in front of the French consulate, having followed the bank of a narrow channel which, just beyond a bridge linking one side of the town to the other, formed a magnificent lake. From the terrace of the consulate we had a wonderful view over the town, with its camels quietly chewing the cud and its people grave and silent as phantoms; and over the lake, whose banks were a sportsman's paradise and whose water was so clear that we could watch the fishes darting among the weeds and pebbles. At the sound of a shot, great clouds of ducks flew up to darken the sky and a score of flamingoes streaked the air with glorious color, wheeling round the lake before coming back to settle in their old haunts. Such a sight aroused all our sporting instincts, and with the consul's help an expedition was quickly arranged. A guide would take us out through the country behind the town to the far shore of the lake, where a boat would be waiting to bring us back.

As usual, our party split into two groups, for Giraud, Desbarolles and Boulanger preferred to wander with pencil and paper through the streets which promised an infinite variety of fascinating things to sketch, while Chancel, Alexandre, Maquet and I shouldered our guns and set out in search of sport, leaving the town by a gate in the great wall, for Bizerta, in the nineteenth century, is fortified as strongholds were in the twelfth. We made our way toward the left and climbed the mountain side, crossing a Turkish cemetery where each man's turban lay at the head of his grave. The higher we went, the wider spread the sea before our eyes, calm, silent and empty, the *Véloce* the only black speck on its azure mirror. Around our feet the land was thick with game, and before we had gone a hundred paces we put up two flights of partridge. Chancel fired and brought down a bird very much like the red-legged partridge we have in France.

Though we saw no one working in the fields, the country looked well tended and fertile, with olive trees growing freely, while here and there a solitary palm towered above them like the rear guard of an uncivilized horde driven back into the desert by the march of progress. Old, rusty cannon stretched their necks through embrasures and looked at us from the tops of fortifications, while now and then on the distant road we caught sight of a galloping horseman or a camel driver. We hunted for about two hours, working right round the town, and seeing at least fifty partridge, shooting five or six. The highest honors for skill, if not for spoils, fell to Alexandre, who astonished our guide by bringing down a lark in full flight.

At the far shore of the lake we found the promised boat waiting for us, manned by two of the crew of the *Véloce*. Maquet and Alexandre decided to walk back through the town, while Chancel and I were rowed toward the middle of the lake to continue our sport. Almost everywhere we could see the bottom, for it is nowhere deeper than six or eight feet and in some places so shallow that we grounded two or three times. I have never seen so much game, and in almost no time at all we shot three or four ducks, a couple of jacksnipe and I don't know how many woodcock.

Suddenly the boat struck an unseen post and sent me overboard head first, to the astonishment of our friends watching from the terrace, who could not imagine what possessed me to jump into the lake fully dressed! Fortunately the water was as warm as if it were summer, though the date was the 4th of December, but the mishap cut short our hunting and we made our way back to the consulate, where I joined the party on the terrace and dried myself as best I could. Soon Giraud, Desbarolles and Boulanger came back from their stroll, their notebooks crammed with sketches. Giraud's were particularly good, and included a fine portrait of the notary of the place and his chief clerk. They had left Maquet and Alexandre in the town, drinking coffee and talking Sabir with a local officer who was obviously delighted to make their acquaintance.

The consul would have liked us to stay, for distractions are rare in Bizerta, except for hunting, which did not seem to interest him, but night was falling and we had to leave. As the ship's boat took up past the quay we stopped to rescue Maquet and Alexandre, who appeared to have made friends with the whole population and had some difficulty in escaping the hospitality offered them by all the men in Bizerta, and perhaps the ladies, too.

While returning to the *Véloce*, we agreed that our visit had made this one of our good days, giving us happy memories of Bizerta, its quiet streets, many of them arcades; its cafés on the waterfront, with camels crouching around their doors; and the friendliness of its people. We climbed on board our ship at about 6 P.M., and at two in the morning, in bright moonlight, we dropped anchor off Tunis.

10

GOLETTA. *French Justice and Turkish Justice*

In the morning we awoke as the *Véloce* fired a salute of twenty-one guns to greet the town of Tunis in the name of the King of France and of myself. (I say "the town," because the Bey was away on a visit to Paris, as we knew.) Tunis, courteous as always, returned our salute, perhaps not as promptly or as correctly as could be wished, but the fault lay with her artillery, not with her good manners.

We were lying in the middle of the gulf, and half a mile off a fine frigate was dancing in the swell, the *Montézuma*, commanded by Captain Cuneo d'Ornano. The weather was magnificent and we had a splendid view of the port, anchored as we were opposite Goletta. Before us lay a long, narrow jetty, just now filled from end to end by a long train of camels and mules, and beyond the jetty a lake on whose further shore stands "White Tunis," as the Turks called her, built like an amphitheater, the houses on the highest slopes silhouetted against the blue sky. To our left rose the fort of the Arsenal and the twin peaks of Bu-Kornain; on our right the Chapel of Saint Louis shone like snow in the sunlight; while behind us, on the far bank of the anchorage, rose the massive, bare, dun-colored mountains where lead is mined.

Tunis was too far away for us to see whether our cannonade had roused the town itself, but we certainly noticed a good deal of commotion in Goletta, a kind of advance post which takes note of passing ships in the name of Tunis. A boat left the jetty and rowed toward us with all speed, bringing out our French consul, M. Gaspari, a charming man who has lived on the far side of the Mediterranean for twenty years and loves playing Providence to any Europeans visiting Tunis for business or pleasure. He has become an antiquary and devotes his leisure to the period between Greek and Roman times and the Middle Ages, between Dido and Saint Louis, Appian and Joinville.

Though we were all agog to reach Tunis, there were certain formalities to observe first, and before Commandant Bérard could go ashore it was his duty to pay a courtesy visit to his superior officer, Captain d'Ornano. (Though the *Véloce* looks quite impressive as she plows in solitary state through the wide, blue Mediterranean, she is a mere infant beside the *Montézuma*.) So we planned to have lunch on board, and then leave the *Véloce* in two separate boats, one to convey Commandant Bérard to the *Montézuma* and the other to take us to the jetty where we would wait for the Captain to join us, spending our time examining M. Gaspari's collection of antiquities, or perhaps trying to shoot flamingo, for ever since I first set eyes on these lovely birds at Bizerta, the day before, I had been longing to bring one down.

We hurried over our meal as much as we could, but on a warship everything follows such a strict routine that I doubt if we saved five minutes, and it was after eleven when we landed on the jetty. M. Gaspari was soon entertaining us in his home, pressing us to try his champagne, his maraschino from Zara, his *resolio* from Florence. At close range, Goletta puzzled us very much, and it is almost impossible to describe the mixed Asiatic and European population thronging the quays. What struck us most forcibly was the appearance of the Tunisian National Guard.

The Bey, as everyone knows, is a lover of Progress, and he therefore decided to have a militia as much like ours as possible. Only two things are needed for such an army—men and uniforms. He already had the men, so he set about getting the uniforms, and imported from France twenty thousand pairs of red trousers and twenty thousand blue tunics, all made for men of average height, namely, five feet four inches. Unfortunately, nothing is more unpredictable than the rate of growth in hot climates, and of the twenty thousand soldiers who were to wear these uniforms, about eight thousand proved to be six or eight inches taller than the average Frenchman, while another eight thousand were only five or five feet two inches. The remaining four thousand with a height of anything between five feet two inches and five feet six inches, conformed roughly to the celebrated "average," and these were the only ones whose uniforms fitted reasonably well.

If such a thing had happened in France we should at once have separated these twenty thousand men into three distinct army corps; one with their trousers and tunics too long, one with them too short, and the third about right. In that way we should at least have obtained some semblance of uniformity. But in Tunis the authorities are not so particular, and consequently the army of His Highness the Bey of Tunis looks extremely odd. Now, to these differences of height, add differences of color and race; add crimson skull caps with silk tassels, gray burnooses, and finally an instrument worn hanging from the belt halfway down the thighs (it looks like a corkscrew, and I never managed to discover what they use it for), and you will have some idea of this celebrated militia.

What struck me next was the number of men rushing about the streets or working in the port wearing cotton nightcaps perched coquettishly on the top of their heads, and I inquired about them. Here is the story I was told. Twenty years ago, during the reign of an earlier Bey, a ship bound from Marseilles to Gibraltar with a cargo of cotton caps was driven by a gale into the harbor of Tunis. At that time every ship entering Tunis had to pay a duty, an arbitrary sum that varied according to the whim of the *raia-marsa*, the harbor master. Naturally, the Captain of the French ship found he had to pay this duty, and, equally naturally, the *raia-marsa* fixed it at an exorbitant sum. It is a hard matter to collect a levy of any sort from the men of Marseilles. They do not forget that their proud city, daughter of Phocea, sister of Rome, rival of Carthage, refused to pay taxes to Julius Caesar! A fine thing, to defy Caesar and then have to pay a mere harbor master! Yet the matter had to be settled before the ship could sail.

The French trader sought an audience with the Bey, threw himself at the feet of this Commander of the Faithful, told his story and begged for justice.

"Do you wish to have justice in the French or the Turkish manner?" inquired the Bey.

The Frenchman pondered for some time, and then, with commendable faith in the legal methods of his native land, replied: "In the French manner."

"Very well!" said the Bey. "Go back to your ship and wait." The Captain bowed to the ground, kissed the royal slipper, returned to his ship and waited. A month went by, two months, three months. The captain went ashore, and as the Bey passed along the road he fell at his feet and cried: "Have you forgotten me, Your Highness?"

"Not at all," the Bey replied. "You are the Frankish captain who came to complain to me about the *raia-marsa*."

"And to whom you promised justice."

"Yes, but justice in the French manner. What do you complain of now?"

"Of having waited these three months for justice, in vain."

"Listen," said the Bey. "Three years ago your consul affronted me and I sent a protest to your King, asking for justice. I am still waiting for a reply. So come back in three years, and we will see."

"The devil!" murmured the Captain to himself, beginning to understand. "What if I had asked for justice in the Turkish manner, Your Highness?"

"That would have been a very different matter. You would have been given satisfaction at once."

"Is it too late to change my mind?"

"It is never too late to learn wisdom."

"Then, *Altesse*, I beg you, let me have Turkish justice."

"In that case, follow me," and the Bey led the way to his

89

palace where he again received the Captain in audience. "What sum did the *raia-marsa* demand from you?"

"Fifteen hundred francs, Your Highness."

"And you think that excessive?"

"At least three times too much, in my opinion."

"You may be right. Take these fifteen hundred piasters, worth one thousand francs. Go and pay your dues."

"Oh, Excellency, you are the very beam of the scales of justice," replied the Captain, prostrating himself to kiss the Bey's slipper. As he rose to depart, the potentate inquired: "Are you perfectly satisfied? Have you nothing else to ask of me?"

"Well, *Altesse,* there is one thing, but I hardly dared to mention it."

"Then do so now, without fear."

"It seems to me that I ought to receive some recompense for the time I have had to waste. Especially," he continued, taking heart as the Bey nodded, "since, if I had reached Gibraltar at the start of the winter, as expected, I should have sold all my merchandise. Now, winter is over, and it is too late."

"What is your cargo?"

"Cotton nightcaps, Your Excellency."

"What are they?" The Captain took a sample from his pocket and showed it to the Bey, who looked at it in bewilderment. "Is it a utensil of some sort? What is it used for?"

"To wear on the head, *Altesse,*" replied the trader, suiting the action to the word.

"It is very ugly," said the Bey pensively, stroking his beard.

"But very comfortable and snug."

"And you say that by keeping you waiting I have caused you loss?"

"To the tune of at least ten thousand francs, Your Highness."

"Then I will see what can be done," and the Bey clapped his hands. His secretary entered and bowed to the ground, whereupon the Bey dictated a few sentences in Arabic (which the seaman did not understand) and ordered: "Publish this decree throughout the town." As the secretary made obeisance and ran to carry out his lord's command, the Captain asked, timidly: "May I know the meaning of your proclamation, *Altesse?*"

"Certainly. I have commanded that, as from tomorrow, no Jew may show himself in the streets of Tunis unless his accursed head is covered with a cotton cap. Offenders to be instantly beheaded. Now go back to your ship, take out your stock and get ready for customers."

Pausing only to kiss the Bey's feet, the Captain rushed back on board and began unpacking his cargo.

Meanwhile there was consternation among the 25,000 Jews in the town. Even the wisest rabbis were not sure what a cotton cap might be, till at last a young fellow recalled that he had once seen a Normandy sailor wearing one. It was a relief to know what the object was, but how could twelve thousand of them be obtained overnight? Grown men clasped their hands and twisted their arms in despair; women tore their hair; children filled their mouths with dust, and they all prayed that the God of Isaac and Jacob, who once rained down manna from heaven, would show them where such things might be found. Suddenly a rumor ran through the crowd: "That three-masted ship in the harbor is full of cotton caps!" "God be praised!" "But would it have enough for everyone?"

They tumbled into boats as though escaping from a ship-wreck till the whole lake was crowded and Goletta was in utter confusion. Five or six boats foundered, but the water was only four feet deep, so no one was drowned. On they went toward the *Notre-Dame-de-la-Garde*, where the captain, having watched events through his glass, was ready. Hundreds of little boats surrounded the ship and twelve thousand voices clamored, shouted frantically for cotton caps, till the Captain made a gesture for silence. "You want cotton caps, gentlemen?" said he, when every sound had died away. "But such articles are greatly in demand at the moment. I have just had word from Europe that prices have soared."

"We know, we know. We are prepared to make sacrifices to get them."

"Listen," said the Captain. "I am an honest man." (The Jews trembled, for that is the phrase they use themselves when about to fleece a Christian customer.) "I will not take advantage of you." (They grew paler still.) "My cotton caps cost me forty sous each, and I will be satisfied with a profit of only a hundred per cent." (Hosannah!) "Here you are, then. Fine cotton nightcaps for only four francs each.

"One moment," he continued, as twelve thousand arms were outstretched. "We must keep things shipshape. Let every man come aboard on the port side and leave to starboard." So each Jew walked in single file across the deck, put down four francs, picked up a cotton cap and went thankfully back to Tunis.

The trader counted his takings—48,000 francs, with a clear profit of 36,000—and on the next day returned to the palace and threw himself at the Bey's feet. "Ah! It's you again," said the Turk. "What do you want this time?"

"I come to offer Your Highness my profound thanks."

"You are satisfied? You prefer Turkish justice to French?"

"Infinitely! There can be no comparison!"

"Wait. You haven't finished yet." Once more the Bey called his secretary, who entered with his hands humbly folded across his breast, bowed, and wrote a fresh proclamation at his master's bidding: "In the name of Sidi-Hussein-Pasha, Bey of Tunis, it is hereby forbidden for any Jew to appear in the streets of Tunis wearing a cotton cap. Twenty-four hours' grace will be allowed to enable him to sell his property, but when this period has elapsed, any offender will be instantly beheaded."

"Your Excellency is the greatest Bey who ever lived!" the captain cried in high delight.

"Then go back to your ship and wait."

Half an hour later, trumpets sounded in the streets of Tunis and the people crowded round the herald to hear the latest edict, all the Jews proudly wearing their cotton nightcaps dangling over one ear. The decree was proclaimed, and the Jews looked at each other in bewilderment. Their first impulse was to throw their caps on the fire, but they are shrewd, and they had twenty-four hours to find a buyer. Better to lose a half, or even three-quarters of the cost, than the whole! So they bargained with the boatmen (last time they had been cheated in the rush), and were rowed out to the ship which was soon as thickly surrounded as before.

"Captain! Captain!" cried twelve thousand voices. "Cotton caps for sale!"

"Pooh!"

"Cheap, Captain! Don't miss this chance!"

"I've just had a letter from Europe! The market has slumped."

"We'll drop our price, too!"

"Well, as I told you, I paid forty sous each for the last I bought, but now I can't pay more than twenty."

Deep groans greeted his offer. "Please, Captain, only thirty!"

"Twenty. Take it or leave it." They still hesitated, and the trader turned his back on them, shouting to his crew: "All hands on deck! Up with the anchor, my lads! We're off!"

The chains of the capstan clanked, the anchor began rising, and the mainsail was half unfurled when at last the sorrowing Jews agreed to the Captain's price. "Good! Hold on, my men! Now," turning to his former customers, "come up one by one on the port side and leave on the starboard." So every Jew returned his cap, collected twenty sous and departed, reflecting that, after all, he had saved his head twice over for a paltry three francs. Not dear!

As for the Captain, he had his cargo back and still retained his profit of 36,000 francs. Being wise in the ways of the world, he took 18,000 francs and went to the Bey's palace.

"Well," said that great man, "do you consider yourself fully recompensed for the delay you complained of?"

"Most generously, Your Highness! Almost too much! I have brought you half my profit."

"Bah! Put it away! Turkish justice is free!"

"Oh! Throne of Heaven!" cried the Captain. "In France, a judge would not have been content with half. He would have taken at least three-quarters!"

"That's where you're wrong! He would have had it all!"

"Oho! I see you know France as well as I do!" The grateful trader prostrated himself in the dust to kiss his benefactor's slipper for the last time, but the Bey gave him his hand. Full of joy, the Captain hurried back to his ship with his 18,000 francs, and a quarter of an hour later he was flying into the distance with every stitch of sail, in case the Bey might change his mind.

The Jews never knew the explanation of those two contradictory decrees, but they philosophically took the whole affair as a tax it had pleased the All Highest to levy upon them. This tax, however, unlike any other, had left them with a pleasant memory. For twenty-four hours they had worn elegant cotton nightcaps, and much preferred them to their customary yellow hoods or black turbans. When the present Bey came to the throne, an occasion when boons are granted, the Jews petitioned to be allowed to wear cotton caps again.

The new Bey saw no objection, and, being a lover of progress, he duly authorized this gracious headgear, which he took to be an essential, characteristic symbol of European civilization. Hence the surprising number of cotton caps I had noticed along the quays of Goletta, but nowadays they are no longer imported, for elderly Turks spend their time knitting them.

❧ ❧ ❧

11

WHITE TUNIS

About two o'clock Commandant Bérard rejoined us in his yawl and our whole party went on together toward Tunis. The channel from the sea to the lake is scarcely twenty-two yards wide and the lake itself is so shallow that only very light boats can pass. The place has a strange atmosphere, like another Dead Sea—its reddish-brown water is said to be poisonous—and the course that boats must follow is marked by posts rising a foot or two above the water. On every post a mournful cormorant is perched with folded wings, still as a bird carved on a tombstone, till a fish swims within reach. Then it dives into the water, reappears on the surface with its prey, resumes its former position and waits for its next catch. These fish, harmless to sea birds, would, I was told, be fatal to any Arab or Christian imprudent enough to eat them, because of the foul water.

Now and then a flock of flamingoes rose from some point on the shore, their long necks and legs fully extended, and flew over the low-lying plain in a line as straight as though it were drawn with ruler and pencil. The single red splash of color on their bodies, like an ace of diamonds, makes them look like playing cards on wings! This whole sheet of water is thronged with birds—gulls, ducks of every species, swimming and diving, disporting themselves with the confidence all wild creatures show in uncivilized countries.

Making our way toward Tunis, which loomed larger each

moment, we passed several heavy boats with their keels in the mud, being forced along by means of poles which the sailors thrust through the shallow water to the lake bottom. After three hours, as night was falling, we reached the end of a long, wide jetty covered with timber and other construction materials and crowded with workmen whose clothes were part European, part Arab, almost all of them wearing cotton caps like those I spoke of just now. These men were from Leghorn, and are called *Gournis* in Tunisia.

On the jetty we were met by M. de Laporte, junior consul at Leghorn, at present acting as deputy for the senior French consul at Tunis, who had accompanied the Bey on his visit to Paris. M. de Laporte had brought his carriage, drawn by two horses and driven by an Arab coachman, but it was not large enough to take us all, so we said we would walk to the town which lay half a mile or so away, its dazzling whiteness already dimmed to gray by the coming night.

Suddenly it was dark, and we experienced something characteristic of the towns on the Orient. Great, ugly masterless dogs, looking part fox, part wolf, came howling around us, their hackles rising, their tails erect and stiff. One of them in particular leapt on top of a long wall and ran beside us barking furiously, ready to jump on us at any minute. Two or three times I had him in the sights of my gun, but M. de Laporte would not let me fire. They left us only when we reached the gates of the town, and I confess I was not sorry to be rid of the snarling pack. Any European rash enough to wander alone at night in this no-man's-land between the city walls and the lake would certainly be devoured.

We were admitted, indeed, almost engulfed, by the dark vaulted gateway that serves as the entrance to Tunis and gives on to a little market place where, on the far side, stands the only European-type house I noticed in the town, a tall building with green Venetian shutters, the residence of the English consul. The French consulate lies a hundred yards further on, typically Moorish, as I was delighted to see, and M. de Laporte made us cordially welcome as his guests for the evening, much regretting that he could not offer to accommodate us all for the night, but begging me, at least to stay until morning.

This French consulate serves as a refuge for men fleeing from danger and seeking French protection; as a tribunal where disputes can be brought to the consul for arbitration; even, if necessary, as a prison. Laporte showed us his judgment seat, a kind of throne covered with three magnificent lion skins, while a fourth lay in front of it as a footrest. In the consulate at the moment were a young Jewess, come to complain of her husband; a prisoner serving a three-day sentence for debt; and a refugee whom Laporte had promoted to be his cook. When we arrived the cook was preparing supper and we could not see him until later in the evening; the prisoner could wait till morning; but the Jewess could be heard at once, so M. de Laporte settled himself on his throne, we all seated ourselves around him, and the plaintiff was brought in.

She was a magnificent creature with her gold-embroidered robes, her almond eyes emphasized with kohl, eyes that gazed at us with the docile yet untamed look one finds only in gazelles and the women of the Orient. Without uttering a word she removed one of her slippers, knelt before the consul and passed him the slipper, turned inside out. We understood nothing of this pantomime which obviously had a definite meaning, but Laporte's expression showed us the matter was serious. He noted her name and address, promised her that justice would be done, and sent her away apparently quite satisfied, whereupon we asked him for an explanation, which I will briefly convey to you, Madame.

You will recall that in Bible times God destroyed Sodom and Gomorrah because of their wickedness, but some of the inhabitants must have managed to escape and perpetuate their race (how, I've no idea), for one hears of their descendants up and down the world, in the Levant as elsewhere, and this woman's husband was of their number. In Tunis, the customary punishment for the first offense is a sharp reprimand; for the second, a fine; and should there be a third the offender is soundly thrashed like a schoolboy whose homework is all wrong. A man who could so ill-treat such a pretty wife as the Jewess we had just seen should have been whipped till the blood ran.

After giving judgment, our host led us in to supper, a really superb meal, and having enjoyed it to the full we asked permission to compliment the chef in person. His name was Taib, and he received our praises with a modest humility that we found quite touching. We asked M. de Laporte how he had managed to find such a treasure of a cook in Tunis, and he replied: "Taib was formerly *chef de cuisine* to one of the greatest lords in this country, but one day he absentmindedly made some mistake or other when creating a sauce, and his master sentenced him to be given five hundred blows with a cudgel. As the tenth blow fell, he managed to slip through the hands of the torturers, fled for his life and took refuge in the French consulate. As long as he stays here and cooks divinely he is safe. If his skill shows any sign of lapsing I have only to threaten to send him back to his former master, and to the 490 strokes still waiting for him there, and his zeal soars to fresh heights."

After supper, M. de Laporte introduced his colleagues, *Messieurs* Rousseau and Cotelle. Their wives were sisters, charming ladies from Smyrna who knew Paris well, and entertained us in their pretty apartments where the furnishings were entirely French, so that we could have believed ourselves back in Paris. The evening hours flew swiftly by as we talked of balls and the opera, Victor Hugo and the Théâtre-Historique,[1] celebrities of the day in literature and art, and lovely Frenchwomen whom we knew—you among them, Madame. It was midnight when we at last said good night to our charming hostesses, and my friends left with their janissary to find their hotel while I was conducted to my room.

Once there, I opened my window, all flooded with moonlight, and found myself back in Tunis. My room overlooked

1. The new theater then being built for Dumas in Paris on the Boulevard du Temple.—*Ed.*

a street where I noticed a pack of wild dogs wandering in search of prey, but the prospect of the whole countryside was calm and majestic. A mighty palm tree stood motionless in the still air, decking with beauty a tiny mosque in the foreground. Beyond lay the lake, where now and then I heard the cry of a marsh bird, and on its further shore Goletta seemed no more than a cloud on the edge of a restless, vague infinity, the sea. To my right stretched the great circle of mountains that form the Bay of Tunis; on my left, Cape Carthage; and if, a short time ago, I had forgotten Tunis for Paris, now I forgot Paris even more completely for Tunis.

* * *

We had agreed to meet at seven o'clock in the morning to explore Tunis on foot, and as we passed through the courtyard Laporte showed us his prisoner. The poor fellow's debt was only 50 piasters, about 34 francs, which we naturally paid so that he could be at once set free. As usual, Boulanger and Giraud were missing. On leaving their hotel they had entrusted themselves to a villainous looking Italian guide, and, sketchbook in hand, had gone off with him, no one knew where.

Laporte kindly offered to show us the town himself so we lost no time in setting out, hoping to discover Boulanger and Giraud en route. The streets of Tunis have no names and the houses no numbers. Should you wish to direct anyone to a particular place, you must indicate as best you can that it is near such and such a bazaar or mosque, café or shop. Europeans cannot own houses in Tunis, they must rent them. Moors can be owners by inheritance or purchase, and if one of them finds his house too small he first obtains permission from the Bey, then builds an archway out from one of his walls, over the street if necessary, and makes himself another room above the arch. If, in the process, he blocks the window of the house opposite, so much the worse for the unfortunate owner of the window.

One of the first things we noticed was a number of handwritten playbills (printing as we understand it being unknown in Tunis), stuck on various walls announcing a performance at the theater that evening. They were playing *Michel et Christine* and *The Deserter*, and our first reaction was of keen irritation. A fine thing, to have come all the way to Tunis and be offered only the *Opéra-Comique* so familiar in Paris! But Laporte soothed us, explaining that the players were protégés of his own, a troupe of children acting under the direction of Madame Saqui. As you can imagine, Madame, tears came to our eyes at the very thought of children traveling six hundred miles from home to bring examples of our literature to dwellers in Tunis, and we promised to attend the performance on condition that we could at once pull down every notice we saw. We would recompense Mme Saqui for any loss of custom, but those frightful handbills quite spoiled the look of Tunis for us.

Nothing can give you any idea of the streets of Tunis. Almost every day some house or other, burned to powder by the fierce sun, collapses in a heap of dusty rubble, and these relics of homes make the town seem extraordinarily sad. Here and there, a fig tree that formerly shaded the patio has been allowed to grow unchecked until its branches thrust themselves through a window or a crack in the outside wall. Sooner or later, storms will buffet the tree and the house will fall in pieces around its knotty trunk, never to be rebuilt.

We passed through many such streets, thronged with ghost-like Moorish women and Jewesses in their striking robes, until we came to a bazaar where we found Giraud and Boulanger taking coffee outside a little Moorish shop. They were already on friendly terms with the proprietor, who, as we arrived, at once had cups brought for us all. His name was Moustapha, and as he spoke Italian, or, rather, lingua franca, we could converse with him freely.

His shop was totally unlike anything we know in France. A Moorish shop is a kind of oven hollowed out of the thickness of a wall, and the proprietor usually stands outside, his pipe in his mouth and his eyes full of dreams, one foot in a slipper and the other bare. Thus he waits for custom, but does not seek it. Indeed, it pains him if a customer intrudes upon his visions of delight, for his pipe usually holds hashish, not tobacco. Here it is the customer, not the shopkeeper, who puts himself out to make conversation, for he needs to buy, but the owner does not need to sell. He tears himself away from his dreams only to name the price for whatever the buyer wants, and at once returns to his reverie. Then you can buy or not, as you will, but do not attempt to haggle. At best he would think it a joke; at the worst he would take it as an insult.

We had arrived at a most opportune time, about midday, when the auction sales begin, and amid an incredible din, coffers, burnooses, sashes, carpets from Smyrna or Tripoli are offered to bystanders. At two o'clock the infernal uproar stops as if by magic, the crowd disperses and business is over. I bought a coffer covered with mother-of-pearl and tortoise shell, as large as those we read of in the *Thousand and One Nights*, in which the Sultanas of Baghdad had their lovers brought to them living and taken out dead. It cost me only 360 francs, and I also bought carpets at a tenth of what I should have paid in Paris.

I watched Moors hawking jewels, walking through the bazaar with their forearms loaded with gold chains, bangles of gold coins, fastenings for *haiks*, chatelaines with hanging charms, all to be sold by weight for they are not new. Such things are not made now, and families live by selling, one at a time, the treasures left to them by their ancestors. To learn the price of any jewel that takes your fancy, you go with the vendor to a valuer (there are three or four in every bazaar), who will handle the gold, weigh the jewel and tell you its worth. Then you may buy without hesitation, for if the valuer has deceived you, even by a fraction, you have only to bring a complaint against him. If your complaint is justified, the valuer may lose his head.

How picturesque these bazaars are! Out of wretched little shops that the poorest French matchseller would despise, come the finest silks of the Orient, lovely with gold thread or hand-embroidered flowers, and all the perfumes of the East. Strollers of every nationality throng the narrow streets speaking their own language, while horses, camels, donkeys and water-carriers force a way through the crowd. We could scarcely tear ourselves away from our friend Moustapha, indeed, nothing I could say would induce Giraud or Boulanger to come with us, so we left them and strolled on.

Suddenly Laporte stopped and said: "Would you like to meet the Sheikh Médine? He is the chief of police here."

"I certainly would! The prefect of police in a Turkish town is someone worth knowing!"

"Then as we are outside his court, let us go in."

We crossed the threshold of a kind of stable and saw a magnificent old man of seventy-five or eighty years, sitting cross-legged on a stone platform covered with matting, smoking a long pipe. His head, lightly veiled in smoke, was superb, and his long white beard contrasted vividly with his black velvety eyes like those of a man of thirty. Laporte explained our visit to him, and had some difficulty in making him understand what I was, for the word "savant" has no Turkish equivalent but *"Taleb,"* which conveys the idea of a man who wanders through the cafés telling stories to amuse the customers, an ink pot thrust through his belt like a dagger.

The Sheikh's welcome was none the less gracious. With his hand at his breast he bowed, said he was happy to see me and called for pipes and coffee while we talked of the peace of Tunis. According to Sheikh Medine, Tunis enjoys angelic calm. No murders and hardly any robberies, except perhaps of Christians or Jews, who do not count. As we conversed, two fine young men in Turkish dress, one aged twenty-five and the other about thirty, came in turn to report to the Sheikh before going on their way. They were his sons, in charge of police affairs under their father's guidance. I was introduced to them and commended to their protection, which, I was told, meant I would be safe anywhere in Tunis by day or night, provided that after dark I carried a lantern and did not venture outside the walls, since the wild dogs were not under the Sheikh's jurisdiction. We passed an hour in casual conversation—I remember admiring a very lovely lamp hanging from the ceiling—then we took leave of our host and continued our stroll.

A hundred yards on, I stopped to admire a wonderful door most delicately carved in wood, and felt a sudden strong urge to possess it. It stood at the entrance to a barber's shop, so I went in and was at once thrust into a chair, while the proprietor offered me a mirror with one hand and seized his razor with the other. Quickly Laporte explained what I wanted while the hairdresser listened with growing perplexity, quite unable to fathom why a foreigner should have come all the way from Paris to seize his shop door. But Laporte was not a diplomat for nothing, and at last the barber took the suggestion seriously, thought a moment or two, and named a price of 1,500 piasters—about 1,000 francs. I at once suspected he was more Jew than Arab, and offered him 200, whereupon he slammed his door in my face. I strongly resented such behavior, but, after all, the man was within his rights, and since a crowd of natives had gathered round, our wisest course was to walk on.

Boulanger and Giraud were still in the bazaar, anxious to show me a hundred things I had missed on my first visit, and it was two o'clock before we returned to the consulate, where a meal awaited us. In the courtyard I found the elder son of Sheikh Médine bearing the lamp I had admired, which the courteous old gentleman begged me to accept. He also brought with him four men carrying the door from the hairdresser's shop as a further present from the Sheikh, which astonished and embarrassed me. Yet the explanation was simple. As chief of police, the Sheikh had been informed of the crowd that collected outside the barber's shop, and on inquiring the cause had learned of my wish for the door and the exorbitant price the owner had asked for it. Accordingly he had commandeered it, and now sent it to me as a pledge of friendship. In the empty doorway he had stationed a sentinel to protect the barber's property till a new door should be made, and since the shop-keeper would have to pay the soldier's wages it was unlikely that he would need to stay long. The temporary inconvenience to the barber was a just punishment for his rudeness to a distinguished visitor.

I felt hopelessly at a loss to convince the Sheikh's son, without offending him, that I could not possibly accept such a gift, but at last, muttering that I was setting a very bad example, and that if such things happened often they would undermine all authority, he allowed me to send the door back to its owner, but for several minutes he kept shaking his head as though to say: "I thought the French were more civilized than that!" Still, he soon regained his friendly manner and with a good grace accepted for himself, his father and his brother, a warm invitation from M. de Laporte to attend a soirée at the consulate on the following evening.

12

❦ ❦ ❦

AT THE PALACE OF THE BEY

We had planned to spend the next morning visiting the ruins of Carthage, but it was not to be. The night before, the Bey of the Camp, who was acting as governor of Tunis while his cousin, the reigning Bey, was paying a state visit to France, summoned Laporte to his presence and received him most courteously, for our countries are not merely allies, but friends. After the usual exchange of compliments, the Bey continued: "There is a French warship in the harbor at Goletta."

"Yes, Your Highness, the *Véloce.*"

"She honored us with a salute of twenty-one guns."

"Which you graciously returned."

"Certainly. I am always pleased to salute your flag. Why has this ship come here?"

"To bring a French savant, *Altesse.* A writer of books, who wishes to see Tunis."

The Bey pondered for some moments, then inquired: "Did this writer, then, hire a French warship for his journey?"

"No, Your Highness. The King, my master, lent it to him."

This was evidently more than the Bey could readily grasp.

"Am I to understand," he persisted, "that the King of France was willing to lend one of his own ships to bring this savant to Tunis? He must be someone important and powerful."

"Yes, Your Highness, I think he is. He has two hundred

and twenty horsepower, anyway, at the moment," chuckled Laporte.

"Then I must see him. Bring him to me here at noon to-morrow."

Fortunately we had brought with us the ceremonial uniforms we wore at the Infanta's wedding,[1] and would be able to present ourselves in full court dress, with knee breeches and swords. The Bey was at Bardo, his fairy-tale residence three or four miles from Tunis, and we drove there through a violent storm of wind that whipped our faces with sand like splintered glass, lifted the hood from our carriage and even buffeted our horse to a standstill more than once.

At first sight, Bardo looks more like a village than the palace of a prince, a haphazard collection of houses, half Moorish, half Italian, most of them with flat roofs, though two or three are built up to a point, and from their midst a slender minaret shoots up like an arrow toward the sky. The whole place swarms with shopkeepers, tailors, shoemakers, itinerant vendors of fruit or tobacco, tradesmen of every sort who feed and clothe the court and garrison, as well as the prince himself. We were received by the Keeper of the Seals, who was waiting for us in the Entrance Hall and conducted us through several fine apartments, explaining pompously that the Bey would give us audience in the French Chamber. Doubtless the prince intended a compliment, and we learned that it was his favorite room, but I must confess we thought his French Chamber looked exactly like a suburban café in Paris, except for its profusion of sumptuous cushions in the Turkish manner. Sofas stood around the walls, and on one of them, cross-legged and wearing all his insignia in diamonds, the Bey of the Camp sat smoking. He seemed surprised at the sight of this new kind of savant, wearing a dozen crosses and decorations on his chest, and I think our appearance impressed him favorably. He greeted us with his hand on his heart, made me sit near him, and commanded his servants to

1. Cf. *Adventures in Spain*, Ch. 6.

bring coffee and pipes for us. Then, after allowing a reasonable time for reflection, he asked for news of my journey to his country.

I told him we had come from France through Spain, and once the ice was broken, conversation flowed freely. What had I seen and done in Spain? I replied that I had the honor to be acquainted with the King of France and our princes, too. The late Duke of Orléans more than once called me his friend; his brother, the Duke of Montpensier, had continued that friendship and had invited me to attend his wedding to the Infanta of Spain, which had just been solemnized in Madrid. Once in Madrid, I wished to see something of Algiers; once in Africa, I could not bring myself to leave without visiting Tunis and the tomb of Saint Louis. I was on my way to pray at that shrine when I learned he had done me the honor of summoning me to his presence, and I had hastened to obey.

All this was translated by the court interpreter, but obviously the Bey could scarcely credit what he heard. A mere *taleb* to be a friend of the heir presumptive, invited to the wedding of a prince of the blood, traveling about in a warship? Giving him a twenty-one gun salute, too, which at all hazards he had returned, rightly or wrongly! All this was so new and unheard-of, so inconceivable, that he would not have believed a word of it if Laporte had not confirmed each of my statements with a nod.

Silence fell as we enjoyed our pipes, filled with Latakia, and our rose-perfumed coffee. Then the Keeper of the Seals addressed me in his turn and I replied as best I could, while the Bey turned aside a little to converse with Laporte. Suddenly I saw his face grow sad, and he breathed a sigh that was almost a groan. We respected his grief without speaking for a few moments, then I asked Laporte why His Highness was troubled, and he replied: "He is very anxious because no news has reached him from His Royal Highness the reigning Bey, who recently set out for France. A great tempest

107

has been raging in the Mediterranean, and he fears that some catastrophe may have occurred."

An idea struck me like a flash. On leaving Algiers, I had brought away a copy of *La Presse* which had just arrived, and this morning had put it in my pocket to read on the way to Bardo. I fancied that the few lines I had glanced at made some reference to the Bey of Tunis, so I took it out, found the place, and read: "This morning the Bey of Tunis arrived in Paris, rather tired from his journey, but otherwise in excellent health." Quickly I passed the paper to Laporte, while the Bey of the Camp watched me closely. Eastern peoples are always puzzled by our vivacity and cannot guess what our gestures mean, for our hands are more nimble than their thoughts. Holding the newspaper before the Bey's eyes, Laporte pointed to the lines and translated them into Arabic.

"Is that really true?" asked the Bey, evidently not entirely sure that our venal press could be trusted.

"Why!" said Laporte. "It's official!"

"And it was the savant who brought the paper here?" The Bey turned to me, his face calm and full of dignity. "Since you are a wise man there is something you must know."

"And that is, Your Highness?"

"Every bearer of good news can claim a reward equal in value to the news he brings. You have given me priceless tidings, and since I know nothing more precious than the Illustrious Order of Nisham, as soon as I have welcomed His Highness my cousin home again I will ask him to bestow it upon you. If I could invest you with it myself, I would do so at once, but only the reigning monarch has this right. Give your address to the Keeper of the Seals." I bowed my thanks and obeyed. "Do you think my cousin will stay long in Paris?"

"*Altesse,*" I replied in true Oriental style, "when visitors of such high degree visit Paris, they find a hundred doors to let them in, but none to let them out." Graciously the Bey waved his thanks, with, I thought, a hint of dismissal in his gesture, so I begged Laporte to express my deference to our noble host, trying to harmonize my actions with his words, and we bowed ourselves from the audience chamber. (To round off the story of the Illustrious Order of Nisham, the reigning Bey did indeed make good his cousin's promise, and I found it waiting for me in Paris when I reached home.)

The Bey whom I met was Sidi-Mohammed, heir to the throne. Twice a year he travels through the realm with a small army, collecting taxes, hence his title "Bey of the Camp," and he, like his more exalted cousin, has absolute power over the life and death of any subject, presiding over his trial should there be one. The uncle of the present Bey claimed that after interrogating a man for ten, or at most fifteen, minutes he knew for certain whether the accused was guilty or not. Should the sentence be death, the Bey would make a horizontal gesture with his outspread hand and utter the word "*kiss,*" whereupon the poor wretch was led out and killed without delay.

In those days, the method of execution varied with the rank of the victim. A common man, an Arab trader, for instance, would be sent to the hangman, who placed him astride a donkey, facing the tail, and led him through the streets, shouting: "Here is such a one, condemned for such and such a crime. Let his well-deserved punishment serve as a warning to others." When the procession reached a certain gate called Bab-el-Souika, a rope was placed round his neck, he was forced to the top of the gateway and thrust off into space, whereupon the bystanders hurled stones at the hangman, especially if he adopted the traditional practice of standing on his victim's shoulders to hasten strangulation.

A man of more exalted rank would be strangled with a bowstring, and the last to be executed in that way was El Chakir, in 1836 or 1837, whose story you may like to hear, Madame. He was brought to Tunis as a young Caucasian slave, and his skill with figures attracted the notice of Ben Hayat, Chancellor of the Exchequer to Bey Hussein, uncle of the present Bey. Ben Hayat particularly needed an arithmetical genius at that moment, because the *bach mameluke*[2] had left the state revenues in chaos. Things were, indeed, so bad that the Bey was in despair. His coffers were empty; he owed vast sums to the Jews; but, a far more serious matter, he was in debt to French commercial houses for two million francs, and feared bankruptcy. He was brooding over his troubles when Ben Hayat came to him and said: "Two million francs, Your Highness? A Bey of Tunis need not concern himself over such a trifle! You shall have the money by tomorrow!"

"Is it possible? But how?"

"I myself will gladly send you 500,000 francs, *Altesse*. See that the three next richest men of your court are told of this and offered the opportunity to show their loyalty by doing likewise."

Ben Hayat was a subtle man and immensely wealthy. The 500,000 francs he promised to the Bey represented less than a tenth of the fortune he inherited from his pirate ancestors, but to produce an equal sum would ruin or seriously cripple his nearest rivals. By noon next day the Bey had his two million francs, and Ben Hayat had three fewer men to fear.

When Ben Hayat recommended his protégé, El Chakir, for the post recently held by the mameluke, Hussein gladly agreed, and the choice seemed excellent. El Chakir, an extraordinarily clever man, organized the country's finances, established the first regular army Tunisia had ever known, and married one of the Bey's daughters. He made one mistake, however, and failed in gratitude to Ben Hayat, the man to whom he owed his good fortune. The rumor reached the Bey that El Chakir was plotting against him, but whether this would have been noticed had he been more grateful, who can say? Perceiving

2. Grand Vizier. The mamelukes, originally Circassian slaves of the Beys, grew so powerful throughout North Africa that they were virtually masters of the country. In 1811, Memehet Ali treacherously slaughtered 470 of them in Cairo and began a campaign to wipe them out. Probably the one mentioned here died in that purge.—*Ed.*

an unwonted coldness in his ruler's manner, he avoided visiting the Bardo and stayed prudently at home, where he was safe from arrest.

It so happened that the French fleet, under Admiral Lalande, unexpectedly put into harbor at Tunis, and Hussein invited El Chakir to attend a reception at Bardo to welcome the Admiral. It was difficult to decline such an invitation without giving offense, and after taking the precaution of confirming the date and time of the reception with the Admiral himself, El Chakir accepted.

Precisely at noon, Lalande entered the palace by one door, El Chakir by another. The Admiral was escorted to a state room and asked to wait a few moments till the Bey could receive him. He was left alone for an hour, and then, very correctly, the officer of equivalent rank in the Tunisian fleet, Assaunah Monali, entered to convey the Bey's apologies for the delay. He had been settling a little family matter, but was now ready to welcome his guest.

No sooner had the doors of Bardo swung together behind El Chakir than he knew he was doomed, but he was a brave man and showed no sign of fear. He was led before the Bey, who was seated in the Hall of Judgment with the whole *diwan* assembled to left and right. In a loud voice, Hussein accused El Chakir of conspiring with his enemies, the Sublime Porte,[3] and ordered the assembled judges to name the just penalty for such base ingratitude. Not surprisingly, they all voted that treachery must be punished by death. El Chakir knew that it would be useless to offer any defense and declared he was ready to die, but begged that he should be allowed to make his peace with Allah and to prepare the bowstring for his own execution. These boons were granted, and after a period of prayer, El Chakir spent several moments carefully soaping the bowstring that was to strangle him, so that it should run smoothly. Five minutes later it was all over, and Hussein was free to entertain the Admiral. This

3. The official name for the government of Turkey, with whom Tunisia was constantly at war.—*Ed.*

was the "little family matter" that the Bey had been settling, and his phrase was strictly accurate. El Chakir was his son-in-law.

In more recent times, execution by strangulation has been discontinued in favor of decapitation, in the case of prisoners of some importance. As soon as the Bey has pronounced sentence, two *boabs*, his personal servants who act as executioners at need, conduct their victim outside the walls of the town, while the waiting crowds rush forward to snatch some relic of the prisoner's clothing as a good-luck charm, so that he arrives almost naked at the place of execution. There his eyes are bound and he is made to kneel, to pray if he wishes. At a sign from the chief *boab* the assistant pricks the man's right side with a dagger, so that he automatically bends toward the right, whereupon one sweep of the chief's long curved sword instantly strikes his head from his shoulders. During the reign of the present Bey, however, capital punishment is almost unknown, and the rare executions that still occur no longer take place at Bardo.

There was at one time a fourth method of execution. In Tunis it was customary to sew an unfaithful wife into a leather sack with a cock, a cat and a viper, and throw her in the lake. This practice was abolished by Monsieur de Lesseps[4] when he was consul at Tunis, and now these pathetic sinners are deported to the island of Kerkennah.

4. M. Matthieu de Lesseps, father of Ferdinand de Lesseps who made the Suez Canal, was consul general at Tunis, where his son joined him as assistant vice-consul in 1828.—*Ed.*

13

❧ ❧ ❧

ARAB AND MOORISH WOMEN

Having broached the subject of the women who live in this part of the world, I will tell you a little more about them, for their customs will be strange to you, Madame.

Women of the nomadic Arab tribes, whose home is the desert, often have strong personalities and exercise considerable influence on their families and communities, but the closer women live to the towns, and consequently to Turkish civilization, the less importance they have as individuals. Mahomet had a perfect understanding of the peoples he was to civilize, and the paradise he promised true believers was entirely sensual. A Moslem is allowed to take four wives, and as many concubines as he can support. An Arab has even wider freedom, for he can divorce his wife at will. People at Mascara could remember a man called Sidi-Mohammed-Ben-Abdallah, a native of Morocco, who in his lifetime of ninety years married ninety wives! Thirty-six of his children were still alive when I was there. The more wives an Arab has, the better off he is. One tends his flocks, herds or camels; others carry wood and water or labor in the home; the newest wife is her husband's favorite, so her tasks are few and light; while his first wife remains in general charge of the household. They are all slaves of indoor life, forbidden to go out unveiled. Never ask an Arab how his wife is, for that would be to insult him! By all means inquire about his home, his aunt, his grandmother, but of his wife, not one word!

The Moorish and Arab women I saw in towns have a strange, arresting beauty, their skin pale and smooth as milk, their large eyes dark and shining. Though they seldom have pretty throats, their hands and arms are charming. In youth they are plump, and in later life fat. Having nothing much to do, they sit drinking coffee, eating sweetmeats, and devoting their whole attention to painting their eyelids and brows, sticking beauty spots on their cheeks, staining their nails, the palms of their hands and the soles of their feet with henna. Almost as soon as their toilet is finished it has to be done again, for they wash themselves three or four times a day. Their gleaming black hair is neatly dressed with Spanish combs, their eyelids shine, and their lashes are heavily outlined with kohl, a preparation each woman makes for herself from wood ash, mixed with mother-of-pearl burned with brightly colored lizards and beetles, all reduced to powder. This she keeps with her in a little bottle of gold, silver or wood, according to her social position. When she wishes to use it, she thrusts into the powder a very smooth, round match stick, then folds back each eyelid in turn over the stick which she pulls sharply to right or left making a firm dark line that adds an exotic brilliance to her eyes.

Eyebrows are defined and given a shapely regularity with Chinese ink, and an Arab poet may well say: "The brows of my beloved are like twin brush strokes drawn by a sure hand." These women keep their bodies (except for their heads) entirely free from hair by covering their skin, once a month or so, with a paste they make from soft soap and orpiment.[1] They smooth it on, step into a bath, and the hair falls away at a touch, so that they look like antique marble statues. As long as they are young and pretty their traditional cosmetics suit them marvelously, giving them a strange fascination, but with age and child-bearing their charms quickly fade.

1. Arsenic trisulfide, found in small quantities as a natural mineral and made into a yellow pigment.—*Ed.*

Their usual dress is a fine, transparent chemise and short, wide trousers of red, blue or green silk reaching to the knees. Below, their legs are bare, and on their feet are embroidered velvet slippers, though when women are sitting at ease their slippers are generally strewn around them on the floor. Rich Moorish women usually wear headdresses, collars and bracelets of gold pieces, sometimes as many as two or three hundred gold coins called *maboules,* and these they never lay aside, not even in their tenderest, most passionate moments. A woman of more modest fortune wears silver coins in the same way. If she is poor, she contrives a much lovelier adornment by threading buds of orange blossom on silk, and so making perfumed garlands for her hair, or bracelets for her wrists and ankles. It goes without saying that none of these women can read or write. The songs they sing are learned by rote; their thoughts are bounded by their material possessions and the pleasures of eating, drinking and making love. We shall meet these Moorish women again at balls in Constantine and Algiers. Meanwhile, let us consider the true Arab women, who know nothing of balls.

Women of the desert tribes, tent dwellers whose food is sparse and simple, are, by contrast, creatures of imagination with a sense of poetry and adventure, inspiring their lovers to deeds of daring. Remember, the desert Arab of today is still the Arab of the thirteenth or fourteenth century, and, like the knights of the Middle Ages, he glories in proving his skill and courage in single combat or in some hazardous enterprise.

In 1825 Hussein ruled the province of Oran, and on one of his visits to collect taxes he encamped beside the river Mina. A young man of the nearby tribe of the Mohals, Hamoud by name, was madly in love with a young Arab girl, Yamina. Plans for their wedding were already settled when Yamina suddenly told her lover that she would not marry him unless, at their wedding feast, she could drink from the Bey's silver cup. Every Arab horseman regards his silver cup as his most treasured possession. It is shaped like a bowl, but has a handle through which is threaded a red or green cord some four feet long, attached to the owner's waist. When fording a river, even at a gallop, he can fill his cup from the stream with a swift rotatory movement and raise it to his lips without spilling a drop.

Hamoud showed no surprise at his beloved's caprice, and at nightfall he undressed on the far bank of the river, opposite the camp, keeping only his hunting belt and his *moun*, a deadly little dagger with a coral-encrusted hilt that, in Bedouin hands, can cut off a man's head. Why did Hamoud go naked? First, because, being copper-colored he could not then be seen in the dark; secondly, because wild dogs do not bark at a naked man, or so the Arabs firmly believe. He swam the stream, knife in hand, then crawled like a snake between the saddles placed, as usual, around the principal tent. Suddenly a man came out of the tent, and Hamoud, recognizing him as the Bey's *chiaouch* or personal servant, instantly took cover behind one of the saddles and held his breath.

The *chiaouch*, quite at ease and in no hurry, seated himself on that very saddle and lit his pipe, enjoying a leisurely smoke while Hamoud stayed motionless. By and by the guard knocked the burning ember from his pipe and it fell on Hamoud's loins, but, like a Spartan, the youth still lay without moving a muscle till the fiery lump grew cold, till at last the *chiaouch* rose and strolled away. Immediately, Hamoud slipped into the Bey's tent, drew a breath or two, raised his head, and saw that the Bey and his men were all asleep. In another instant he had seized the cup, slipped unseen to the bank and was swimming back across the river.

When he reached the far side, he stood up and shouted: "Ho, there you Turks! Look in the Bey's tent and ask what he has done with his silver cup!" This gesture of bravado nearly cost Hamoud his life. The guards awoke, ran to the Bey's tent, saw that his cup had been stolen, and fired a few random shots in the direction whence the voice had come. As Hamoud was dressing, a spent bullet broke his leg, and a cry of surprise and pain escaped him. The Turks crossed the river, found the youth lying in his own blood and brought him to the Bey, who demanded an explanation of the theft and especially of his temerity. So Hamoud told Hussein his love story, and Yamina's wish to drink from the Bey's silver cup, whereupon the Bey was so struck by his daring that he gave him the silver cup and 200 duros as well, had him tended by his own surgeon and carried back to his home. Three months later the lovers were married, and Yamina was able to drink from the Bey's cup, which had almost cost Hamoud his life.

Despite such imaginative fancies, an Arab woman's sole aim in life is to please her husband, to fascinate him with her coquetry. Should her fancy stray to a lover, then in her eyes he becomes the noblest man in all the world, and for him she will brave any dangers. If the husband's jealousy is aroused, the tradition of Othello, terrible as it is, is less terrible than the reality. But, almost always, jealousy is powerless against the subtle schemes of passionate lovers, and, in spite of the leather sacks we spoke of, in spite of the ever present risk of death by the knife or by strangulation, adultery is more common among the Arabs than anywhere else in the world.

An Arab may fall desperately in love with a woman whose face he has never seen, attracted by her figure, her reputation for beauty, or because of a private word from some Jewish hawker who has chanced to see her unveiled. Then the gallant employs an *adjouza* (as a procuress is called in the Sahara), who contrives to talk privately with the girl, telling her of the young man's passion, praising his prowess as a hunter or in battle. Since men do not cover their faces, women know them by sight, and the girl is in no doubt of her lover's identity. If he is rich, the *adjouza* will bring presents from him, headdresses, necklaces, bangles, even gold coins, for an Arab woman may accept such gifts without shame.

If the lady accepts his love tokens she gives him a rendezvous at the fountain or in the closer intimacy of her tent,

117

possibly even in her *atouche*, those little curtained shelters in which women travel long distances over the desert on the backs of camels. Such meetings are arranged with the most subtle precautions against discovery, for if the lovers were found together her husband would instantly slay them both.

If she refuses (she may be virtuous or her suitor may not please her), she is still in danger. It is by no means unusual for a flouted lover, hot with wounded pride, to swear to kill the girl who repulsed him, and to keep his oath. She may warn her husband and brothers, who will guard her closely and wait to butcher the would-be murderer as he worms his way into her tent. But if he delays till her peril seems over, and chooses a dark, rainy night when the guards have relaxed their vigilance, he may still succeed in burying a dagger in her breast and escaping unperceived. Sometimes, they say, a romantic woman will drive her suitor to this extreme to test his love and strength of purpose. When, full of passionate hate, he comes to kill, he is received with warm, welcoming arms and stays to love.

Unlike the women of western Europe, Arab and Moorish women accept without question that man is their superior whom they must obey. However, any hint of a threat or undeserved lack of respect often calls forth their vengeance.

Khadidja, daughter of Osman, Bey of Oran, had a lover named Bougrada who, while with her one day, said in lordly fashion that she was his handmaid whom he could destroy if the fancy took him.

"You are wrong to say so," she replied, "and I do not fear you. On the contrary, it is we women who, when we choose, can give life or death."

"Bah! Allah alone has that power."

Scarcely had he spoken when they heard the Bey approaching along the gallery, a very big man who walked with a heavy tread. Bougrada shook with fear. To be found there by Osman would cost him his head. But Khadidja calmly hid her lover in a great chest of mother-of-pearl and tortoise shell that stood in the room. As the Bey entered and glanced

118

around for a seat, she gestured toward the coffer, where he settled himself for a light-hearted chat with his daughter whom he greatly loved.

Suddenly Khadidja turned the conversation to a superb yataghan that hung in a gold scabbard from her father's waist. "Tell me," she said. "Is it really true that your yataghan can cut through iron?" "Certainly!" "I don't believe it," she scoffed gently. "I'll wager it would take at least two blows to sever even the lid of the chest you are sitting on." "One will be quite enough," the Bey replied, rising and preparing to make good his boast.

But Khadidja stayed his upraised arm. "There, there!" she laughed. "I'll take your word for it, father. Do not spoil my pretty coffer that came from Tunis!" So the Bey sheathed his sword and they talked of other matters till, ten minutes later, he went away. Then the young girl drew Bougrada, half-dead, from the chest, and murmured to him: "Oh, my love and light of my eyes! Be wiser henceforth, and never deny that women are all-powerful!"

* * *

I will tell you one more story about women, Madame, a little adventure that happened to me on the day when M. de Laporte and I were received in audience by the Bey of the Camp.

It was three o'clock when we returned from Bardo, too late to visit the ruins of Carthage as we had planned, but we still had time to go and see the *Marabout* of Sidi-Fath-allah. A *marabout* is a holy man, a hermit, and the name is also used for his tomb or dwelling place, often a little stone hut with a round roof. One sees many of them on the outskirts of towns, and some far out in the desert. They serve as a place of sanctuary, and if a fugitive from justice reaches a *marabout* no one may kill him there. (The authorities may, however, and frequently do, surround the place with guards to prevent his escape, give him a loaf and a pitcher of water, and then wall up the only door.) A debtor cannot be arrested in a *marabout*, though his creditor may fix an iron ring to the wall and tie the debtor to it. In the Sahara, *marabouts* are halting places for caravans, a shelter where lost travelers find a free hostelry for the night. Rich men place offerings there "for the love of Allah," dates, figs, unleavened bread, flour, and the poor can eat these provisions to satisfy their hunger, but woe to any man daring to carry away a single fruit, even a pinch of flour! He would surely perish on his journey.

A living *marabout* may earn or inherit the right to be regarded as a saint, for in Africa religious nobility is hereditary, just as titles are with us. Men come from ten, twenty, a hundred miles around to consult a well-known *marabout*, praying him to send them rain or fine weather, the favor of the sheikh or the love of a lady. They go away proudly wearing round their necks or arms the amulets he gives them, generally scraps of parchment bearing verses from the Koran. An Arab trader I spoke to had one which said: "God permits business but forbids usury." Our janissary wore this strange device: "Marriage is like a besieged fortress. Those outside strive to enter; those inside long to get out." (I asked him if he was married, and he replied that his amulet had brought him luck, for he was still a bachelor.) *Marabouts* heal certain diseases by prayer or by touch, cure barren women, ensure the increase of flocks and herds. The greatest of all these holy men was Sidi-el-Hadji-Abd-el-Kader-el-Dje-lali, who had the gift of restoring sight to the blind and whose tomb is at Baghdad, though shrines called *Koubbahs* have been built in his honor throughout Algeria.

Sometimes a *marabout* is a frightful rascal, but his prestige is not lessened thereby, for a Moslem is a fatalist and explains all things as the will of Allah. The last *marabout* who lived in Tunis was greatly venerated. He used to ride through the streets on a tiny donkey with bells on its harness, and when he died he was buried in the mosque itself, the Bey and all the important people of the town attending his funeral. Everything the holy man possessed, even his staff and his little donkey, was bought for fantastic sums by true believers.

At the time of our visit, no *marabout* for miles around stood higher in public favor than Sidi-Fathallah, whom we were going to see. His devotees gave him a name meaning "God opens the gates of happiness," and credited him with almost miraculous powers of curing women of sterility. The rites to be followed seemed to us quite remarkable. A hundred yards from the little village where he lives there stands a rock about sixty feet high, and one side of it is a smooth slope. A woman seeking the blessing of fruitfulness must slide from top to bottom of this slope twenty-five times; five times face downward, five times on her back, five times on her left side, five on her right, and the last five head first. Having performed this ritual, she spends an hour praying with the *marabout,* and if she is young and pretty her curse is usually charmed away so effectively that she returns home with her prayers well on the way to being answered.

We drove to the village in Laporte's carriage and stopped at a pleasant café, where Giraud sketched a group of Arabs in the doorway while Laporte and I drank a cup of coffee inside. Then, leaving the horse and carriage with the landlord, we strolled toward the miracle-working rock, taking care to approach it without being seen. Four women were gravely sliding down the slope, one of them having reached the stage of coming down head first, and we soon understood why Laporte had urged us to keep out of sight, for the moment they set eyes on us they all fled, screaming. Our presence there was almost a sacrilege, and for our own safety it was vital to quiet their cries. Fortunately a young goatherd was watching his flock nearby, and Laporte sent him to assure the women they had nothing to fear from us. One of the gentlemen who had unwittingly disturbed them was the French consul, one a great painter, and the third a learned doctor. (I was the "doctor," there being no equivalent of "writer"!) The women made no reply, but they stopped screaming. Victory was half won! Then, after two or three minutes we saw them peeping at us round the corner of a house, and our victory was complete.

Clearly, they were poised to flee at the least sign of danger, so we made no move, except that Giraud sat down and began a picture of the village with the sea in the background, a blue sheet of water with white-capped waves. Ah, Madame! Women are the same the whole world over! When they saw that we were paying them no attention they grew interested in us, and sidled nearer, one step at a time, till they could peep over Giraud's shoulder. They showed delight on recognizing the outlines of their village in his sketch, and burst into gusty laughter as Giraud's pencil drew the holy rock with them upon it, sliding down in the various conventional positions.

Till now, our visitors had remained veiled, but gradually an eye appeared, then another, a nose, a mouth with teeth like pearls, and finally their faces. Three of the ladies were charming; the fourth, a woman of thirty, looked yellow and ill, her feet and legs much swollen. Laporte spoke a few words in Arabic and her three companions fled, but she held her ground and answered him. The poor woman had taken seriously Laporte's jest that I was a doctor, and wished to consult me. She made no resistance when I lifted her hand to feel her pulse (it was very rapid and she seemed feverish), and seeing her so unconcerned the three young girls regained their confidence and drew closer, giggling behind their hands.

The youngest of them was certainly not yet twelve years old, and her ingenuous, unawakened look made it plain that she knew nothing of love. She had been sliding on the rock simply for fun. I talked with her a little, Laporte acting as interpreter, and asked who her parents were. She was an orphan. But how did she live? As the birds did, on flowers and dew. Yet, poor as she was, she was tidy and clean, her eyelids and nails neatly painted, and her lips so red and bright that they seemed painted too.

I asked her whether, since she had no ties in her own land, she would like to come with me.

122

"Where?"

"To the other side of that great sheet of water," said I, waving my arm toward the sea.

"But beyond the water there is only the sky."

"There's another country over the sea," I told her. "The ships you sometimes see come from that land."

She thought a while, then asked: "And what should I do there?"

A disturbing question, so I replied simply: "Whatever you like."

"Should I have red trousers with gold embroidery, a silk bodice, a cap with sequins and a beautiful *haik* of camel hair?"

"Yes, you should have all those things."

She looked at her friends. "I would go with him," she said.

"What? You would come just like that? Without even knowing me?"

"You are a learned man," she answered. "Since God has given you knowledge, he must also have given goodness."

I turned to Laporte incredulously. "Would she really come?"

"Upon my word, I think she would!"

After a moment's pause, I said: "Have you finished your drawing, Giraud? Then let us be going." From my pocket I took a handful of little silver coins as thin as paper. "Here, my child," I went on. "These will make you a bracelet." Her eyes sparkled with delight, though she scarcely believed I meant it till I poured the coins into her hand. Her cry of joy rang in my ears as I turned away with a sigh for her youth, her sweet springtime of life. Five or six days later, I turned to Giraud and said: "Make me a portrait of her for a souvenir." He took his pencil and drew her on the instant, without needing to ask me who I had in mind.

123

14

❧ ❧ ❧

CARTHAGE. *A Ball in Tunis*

The next day promised to be a very full one, for in the morning we were to visit the Chapel of Saint Louis and the ruins of Carthage, then spend the afternoon aboard the *Montézuma*, and finally attend a great ball to be given that evening at the consulate.

Outside the town gate, at seven in the morning, we took our seats in a carriage driven by a Maltese, who, like a Spanish *zagal*, ran beside his horses instead of traveling on the vehicle with his passengers. The first thing we noticed as we left Tunis was a beautiful *khoubbah*, said to be the tomb of the last Abencerrage,[1] so I stopped the carriage, dismounted, and with my knife carved on its wall the name of Châteaubriand. It was in the country around Tunis that most of the Moors settled when they were driven out of Spain, the land they still regard as their own lost paradise, and I heard of a family living in this neighborhood that still treasured the key of the house their ancestors once owned in Granada.

We drove on into the country as quickly as we could, for it must be confessed that the stench around the walls of Tunis

---

1. The Abencerrages were a family, possibly also a political group, said to have held a prominent position in the Moorish kingdom of Granada in the fifteenth century. After the fall of Granada their descendants settled in Tunis. Dumas' action was in recognition of Châteaubriand's novel about this family, *Le Dernier Abencérage*, published some years earlier.—*Ed.*

is offensive beyond words. (The authorities refuse to clear the sewers and rubbish heaps, claiming that the smell is a protection against plague!) The country itself is almost desolate, though the soil is fertile enough, for in this land of despotic rule no man can be sure that his fields will not be filched from him, so he does not plow or sow. A few olive trees stand here and there, but they are old, bearing little if any fruit, and no new ones are planted.

After three-quarters of an hour we halted at a Moorish café, picturesque as all such places are, their white walls generally shaded by a dark green tree, the proprietors chatting with their customers and the passers-by, while beggars draped in rags wait at the roadside for alms and superbly mounted horsemen gallop past. It was a picture to delight the soul of an artist or a poet, and I wished that Giraud and Boulanger had been with us. They had preferred to spend the morning sketching in Tunis, but would rejoin us later on the *Montézuma*.

Having enjoyed our coffee we shouldered our guns and strolled on through a landscape that grew wilder with every step we took. Relics of ancient buildings still litter the fields with stony mounds, or protrude like bones through the very furrows; broken aqueducts stand like the legs of demolished giant statues. Carthage, that mighty city of legend and history, has utterly vanished from sight, though we could sense its desolate ruins all around us.

Historians tell us that, a thousand years before the birth of Christ, it was founded by a band of fugitives from Tyre, who gave it the Phoenician name of *Kartha-Haddad*, which means "new town"; later, the Greeks knew it as *Karchedon*, and the Romans as *Carthago*, their most dangerous rival, the subject of old Cato's fierce rallying cry, "*delenda est Carthago*." According to Virgil it was not founded till the year 822 B.C., but he also differed from the historians by making its queen, Dido, the contemporary of Aeneas and enshrining their love story in the *Aeneid*. Her real name was Elissa, but because of her travels she became known as Dido, which means "the wanderer." She was the daughter of Belus, King of Tyre, and on his death should have ruled the kingdom jointly with her brother, Pygmalion, but that prince determined to seize the throne for himself. He murdered his sister's husband, Sychaeus (who, as high priest of Hercules, had amassed great riches), hoping to steal his gold. Dido, warned in time, took the treasure and fled over the sea with her courtiers and faithful soldiers, first to Cyprus, then on to Utica on the coast of Africa, where the Tyrian colony gladly welcomed her as their queen.

From a neighboring chief, Iarbus, Dido bought "as much land as could be enclosed by the skin of an ox," on which to build her home. Having sealed the bargain, Dido sought out the largest bullock in all the country round, had it killed, and cut its hide into such fine strips that when joined they reached right across the promontory from the Lake of Tunis to the seashore, and so enclosed a space large enough for her new town, *Kartha-Haddad*. (The very name of the citadel, *Byrsa*, means "leather" in Greek.) Dido's colony prospered so much that Iarbus coveted it, demanded the queen's hand in marriage, and on her refusal led his armies against the town. Forced to choose between the destruction of her people and marriage with a man she loathed, Dido begged for a short delay, had her servants erect a huge funeral pyre, and stabbed herself to the heart upon it, before the eyes of her subjects. For eight hundred years, Punic Carthage grew in wealth and power till Scipio burned it to the ground in 146 B.C.; Roman Carthage, raised from the ruins, also flourished for eight hundred years but was at last destroyed by the Arabs under Hassan, the Gassanid governor, never to be rebuilt.

Amid the ruins of Roman Carthage stands a monument like an Arab *marabout*, the tomb of Saint Louis. Doubtless the similarity in shape is intentional, expressing the present-day Arab view that the French saint is as worthy of veneration as any holy Moslem. It was in 1270 that King Louis IX, loved far beyond the borders of his own kingdom for his perfect chivalry and saintliness, set sail from Aigues Mortes on July 1 to lead his second crusade, landing at Carthage seventeen days later. At that time a Moorish prince was trying to rebuild the town—it was the period when Moorish architecture was at its zenith—and several houses already stood among the ancient ruins, while a fine new castle crowned the hill of Byrsa. The crusaders attacked; laid waste the city, scarce risen from its former ashes; seized the castle and looked on toward Tunis.

Tunis, however, was strongly fortified, the home of 150,000 seasoned warriors. Attack was out of the question until the arrival of reinforcements led by the King's brother, Charles of Anjou, King of Sicily, so Louis encamped around the castle and waited. It was early August, and day after day the fiery sky blazed down upon the burning earth—the very stones too hot to touch, while the sea itself seemed molten lead. The Moors in Tunis had strange instruments of war that hurled clouds of burning sand in the path of the prevailing desert winds blowing over the crusaders' camp, so that fire rained down on them day and night. Then plague broke out in the stricken army and men died in hundreds, so many that the living could no longer bury the dead. The leaders fell beside their men—Count Montmorency, Count Nemours, Count de Vendôme. The King's beloved son, the Duke of Nevers, died in his arms, and at that moment Louis himself was seized with the first pangs. Knowing death was near he lay on a bed of ashes, his arms crossed on his breast and his eyes uplifted to heaven, while the remnant of his army formed a circle round their king. Far out to sea, white sails glittered in the sunshine like a flock of gulls as Charles' fleet at last came in sight, bringing the reinforcements Louis had longed for. Soon their joyous fanfares of greeting could be heard on shore, and at five o'clock in the afternoon of August 25 their leader stepped to land, to be met with the sad tidings of his brother's death two hours earlier.

For 560 years not even a cross marked the place where Saint Louis fell. Then in 1829 Charles X opened negotiations with Hussein, through the French consul, for permission to erect an altar there. The Revolution of 1830 caused further delay, but when Louis-Phillipe (himself a descendant of the saint) came to the throne he sent out an architect, M. Jourdain, with orders to find the exact spot where Louis had breathed his last and erect on it a mausoleum to his memory. Unfortunately, no amount of research could determine precisely where the saint had died, so M. Jourdain and Jules de Lesseps together chose the finest site in the whole region and built the tomb there, on a hill still strewn with broken marble pillars and scraps of mosaic pavements, possibly relics of the very castle where Louis spent his last days.

As we stumbled up the stony hillside a wonderful panorama spread itself before our eyes: to the north, the sea, sparkling in the sunshine; to the east, the promontory of Mercury; to the south, Tunis, white as a city hewn from chalk; to the west, a plain tufted with little dome-shaped hills, each crowned with a *marabout* or an Arab village. We entered the precincts of the monument, noticing that the encircling walls were built chiefly of fragments from the ruined town, broken columns, vases, pieces of sculpture, among them part of a very lovely statue. The interior is beautifully carved in the Arab manner, the work of a Tunisian artist whose name is Younis, as I was told by the custodian, an old soldier of France. There is little else to see. Much to meditate on, perhaps, but meditation is difficult in the company of five or six people. At this moment, as I sit writing at my desk in my study above the noisy streets of Paris, torn between my memories of yesterday and the crowded events of today, I would give a great deal to be able to spend two quiet hours dreaming alone by the portal of Saint Louis' tomb.

As we wandered down toward the shore, the only visible sign of life was a half-naked Arab tilling a narrow strip of soil, goading along two puny oxen yoked to an ancient plow. At the water's edge, a few broken columns of red or white marble rolled to and fro in the swell; further out, waves were breaking over the long black line of a derelict jetty; while dominating the whole desolate scene was the little Arab village of Sidi-bu-Said on the crest of a lofty cliff. How I wished our two painters were with us! What a picture Giraud's lightning perception would have made of this memorable place! How

Boulanger, with his profound melancholy of spirit, would have captured its wild emptiness! I sauntered away to be alone awhile, and lay on the beach, dreaming of Carthage, so glorious in her time, so eloquent in her ruin; hearing in the breakers an echo of cries from centuries ago.

My reverie was cut short by a call from Alexandre, and as I rose I saw a boat signaling to us from a jetty half a mile away. The Captain of the *Montézuma* had sent his yawl to bring us on board for lunch. We walked toward it along an old ruined quay and around two great excavations where three or four snipe were dabbling about in the mud and reeds. Scholars tell us these were the two ancient harbors of Carthage, one for trading vessels, the other for ships of war. The entrance to the port was only sixty feet wide and could be closed by iron chains.

Oh! If I were not afraid of boring you, Madame, there are a thousand tales of Carthage I could borrow from historians of the past! Instead, I will tell you something that may interest you more, for you will certainly remember our old friend Yusuf, that gallant, brilliantly clever soldier. It was from this harbor that he set out for France one fine evening in October, 1830, after a certain love affair that perhaps I ought not to mention, now that he is married to a young and lovely *Parisienne*. But there! Travelers are so indiscreet! That is the price they pay for being entertaining, and I confess I would rather be indiscreet than boring!

One day our French consul, M. Mathieu de Lesseps, saw a fine young man of twenty or twenty-two arriving at the consulate, dressed in the Arab robes he had worn all his life, though he was born in Leghorn or on the island of Elba. It was Yusuf, an officer of the *bach mameluke* and a favorite of the Bey Hussein. Like a story in the *Arabian Nights*, this humble commoner had dared to raise his eyes to the Princess Kabousah, daughter of the Bey, who returned his affection, though all the traditions of the Orient placed a barrier between them. By ill luck it happened that when the young man ventured for the first time into the princess' suite he was seen by a slave who ran to tell the Bey what he had discovered, testifying on oath that it was true. As this slave left the Bey's apartments he had to pass along the corridor by Yusuf's room. The officer was waiting for him and dragged him inside. Behind the closed door there was a clash of arms, followed by loud cries, then silence.

Two hours later Princess Kabousah received a basket of flowers. Under the blossoms she found a hand, a tongue and an eye, with a note saying: "I send you the eye that spied upon you, the tongue that slandered you, and the hand that testified against you." She could make no reply, for Yusuf had already fled to the French consulate.

M. de Lesseps had known Yusuf for a long time, and held him in high regard. He hastened to send him to his own country house at Marsa, on the coast, and instructed his son Ferdinand, who today is the French ambassador at Madrid, to take charge of the fugitive and make sure he escaped safely. Three days later the dinghy of the corvette *La Bayonnaise* arrived to fetch Yusuf, but the Bey's men were guarding the coast line to arrest him the moment he appeared. Yusuf drew the yataghan he could use so skillfully and would have fought his way through, though the odds were ten to one, but M. Ferdinand de Lesseps restrained him, and, flanked by French coast guards, walked close beside him to the shore so that, protected by the consul's son, Yusuf was able to board the corvette unharmed, taking with him a letter from M. Mathieu de Lesseps to Marshal Clauzel[2] which opened for him the career which he has followed so gloriously ever since.

* * *

2. Count Bertrand Clauzel (1772–1842) was one of France's most distinguished generals, who was honored by Napoleon, served in the Peninsular War, sat in the Chamber of Deputies, and after the Revolution of 1830 was made head of the Army of Algiers. Under his patronage, and later under General Valée, Yusuf won renown for his feats of daring in the Algerian campaign, particularly in the assault on Bona in 1832, and was fêted in Paris (1835-1836) where Dumas met him personally. Later, Yusuf became a general and was stationed in Algiers, where Dumas saw him again. (Cf. Ch. 19.)—*Ed.*

The wind had freshened, and the white-crested waves rolling in the bay presented us with a serious problem. To hoist a sail was to risk capsizing; to rely on the oars would mean arriving on the *Montézuma* tomorrow instead of today. However, the decision was not left to us. Sailors are punctilious in obeying orders, and the crew of the yawl had been told to bring us on board by one o'clock. It was now twelve-thirty; the sail might get us to the *Montézuma* in half an hour, so up went the sail. If we capsized, it would be in the course of carrying out instructions, and no one would be to blame.

Instantly the little craft canted over alarmingly, our starboard gunwale awash, our port side five feet in the air with all of us hanging over it in the hope of righting her, but without avail. The flying spray covered us with diamond drops, now and then we shipped a wave, and though we laughed and joked it was with many a longing glance toward dry land, till after three-quarters of an hour we gained the lee of the *Montézuma*, and her huge bulk took the wind from our sail. Compared with her, the *Véloce* is a mere skiff, outclassed by 180 horsepower, and I felt quite humiliated on her account, as well as on my own.

M. Cunéo d'Ornano gave us a cordial welcome as we went on board. With him we found M. and Mme Rousseau, M. and Mme Cotelle, and M. and Mme Sainte-Marie, all of whom we had already met at the consulate, and we much appreciated M. d'Ornano's kindness in affording us an opportunity of seeing them again. Mme de Sainte-Marie, a charming *Parisienne*, came here six or eight years ago with her husband, a captain in the Engineers, when he was sent out to take charge of a government survey of the Regency. The Moors do not take kindly to any scientific exploration of their territory, for they can never believe that a government would send an official, equipped with complicated instruments, to draw maps and make incomprehensible calculations, with nothing more sinister in mind than the advancement of knowledge. However, the French are held in such respect, I would even say affection, in this part of Africa that the reigning Bey gave M. de Sainte-

Marie full authority to make his survey, and even sent a mameluke with an official permit to accompany him for greater security.

With this mameluke, his own inflexible determination and his amazing courage, M. de Sainte-Marie has carried out almost incredible expeditions, discovering lakes and mountains previously unknown, tribes whose very existence was unsuspected, even by the Bey himself. Every now and then he disappears and is not heard of again for months, till one fine day or night he unexpectedly arrives home from Djebel-Auctar or Djebel-Korra. If his wife asks whether he has been in any danger he simply shrugs without answering. For him, life itself spells danger, no more in one place than another. Only from his mameluke does one learn of the attacks made on him and beaten off, the wounds he received, the hunting he enjoyed. He never mentions his adventures himself. After a rest of eight or ten weeks he will vanish for another five or six months. We were fortunate to arrive in Tunis between two of his eclipses.

Lunch on the *Montézuma* was a feast, and the sea air so sharpened our appetites that we did full justice to it. Afterward we were taken all over the ship, and the Captain, rather at a loss to find entertainment for the ladies, ordered a salute to be fired in their honor. They were even shown how to fire a cannon themselves, a thirty-six pounder, no less!

About five o'clock we said good-by to the Commandant, settled ourselves in the dinghies and set out for the shore. The sea was still so rough that we almost despaired of reaching Goletta, but once we were through the channel and on the lake our passage was so calm that we took a shot or two at the great sea birds flapping lazily across the water. With our French crew and French companions, all of us singing French songs, we could have fancied ourselves at home, a picnic party on Lake Enghien, except that Tunis lay in clear view ahead of us. As we set foot on the mole we were met by a crowd of Jews in cotton caps with designs on our purses, and howling dogs with designs on our legs, but we managed to preserve both and reached the consulate without mishap.

There, however, a fresh embarrassment was waiting for us. Word had spread of our purchases from various traders the day before, and the courtyard now looked like a bazaar. Jewelers, carpet-sellers, vendors of silks, mirrors, guns, daggers, pistols, had spread out their wares to tempt us, and the moment we appeared at the gate the whole crew surged forward and engulfed us. But for our two janissaries we should have been torn limb from limb. We shouted at the tops of our voices that the consulate was supposed to offer sanctuary, and Laporte came to our rescue. Finally we all agreed on a truce; tonight should be ours, tomorrow morning we would give some time to these Tunisian merchants, and on that understanding they departed, trustfully leaving their goods where they lay, under the protection of the French flag.

It was already eight o'clock and the ball would begin at nine. Laporte just had time to supervise the lighting of his reception rooms while we dressed, and at nine precisely a French orchestra began a program of quadrilles and polkas. Thirty or forty ladies in tulle and satin danced as best they could with their escorts in black dress suits, while five or six Moors sat cross-legged and motionless in a corner, dignified and splendid in their long robes, looking like a group of masqueraders at a fancy dress party in Paris. But there was much to remind us that we were in Tunis; the porcelain-tiled floor on which Alexandre slid at full length while dancing a polka; the all-pervading aroma of coffee, *chibouques* and hookahs; the sherbet and ices with unfamiliar Eastern flavors.

There was the majestic figure of the Sheikh Medine seated cross-legged on a cushion, his tall sons standing one at each side of him, dutifully observing the respectful custom which in this country forbids children, no matter what their age, to be seated in their father's presence. There was even an Arab storyteller to entertain the guests, and while most of our friends were dancing a few of us listened enthralled to his

133

tale of Prince Charming. It was new to me and I think you would enjoy it too, Madame, though I cannot tell it with the sublime artistry of Hassan-ben-Mahmoud-Djelouli, or of the interpreter who translated it for us, phrase by phrase.

Once upon a time there was born in Tunis a prince so ugly, so incredibly ugly, that with one accord the whole court bestowed on him the name Bou-Ezzin, "Prince Charming." So that the prince should never know of his affliction, the Bey banished every mirror from his son's apartments and forbade anyone to bring such a thing within the prince's reach, on pain of death. The prince grew up happy and well content with his appearance, for naturally his courtiers assured him he was as handsome as any man in the whole realm.

When the young prince reached his twentieth year the Bey died, leaving his kingdom to his son, and since Prince Charming adored his father he resolved to have his beard shaved as a sign of mourning. He therefore summoned a barber, but it chanced that the one who came was a poor devil who had just arrived in the town from Sousse and knew nothing of the palace ban on mirrors. He brought one with him, and before the *bach mameluke* (Grand Vizier) could leap forward to prevent this totally unexpected breach of the law he had placed the mirror in Prince Charming's hand, as for any other customer. So, for the first time in his life the prince saw his own reflection. He gave a cry that was heard from the palace all the way to Algiers, threw the mirror from him so that it broke into a thousand pieces, burst into bitter tears and tore his beard in sorrow, for he realized that he was hideous. Seeing his master acting thus, the Grand Vizier also wept bitterly and tore his beard, so that the palace was filled with their lamentations.

But Prince Charming was a lad of good sense, and after he had wept and torn his beard all day long he reflected that weeping would make him look uglier still, and to tear his beard would mean that more of his face would show. So toward evening he dried his tears, and next morning, though he sighed bitterly and was most unhappy, he had regained his composure.

134

His *bach mameluke*, however, was by no means as philosophic as the prince. He was weeping louder than ever and had plucked out a third of his beard. Prince Charming was deeply touched by his minister's devotion, and day after day he urged the *bach mameluke* to console himself, but all to no avail.

At last the prince, now quite recovered, sent for his Grand Vizier, who entered the royal presence in floods of tears, his beard completely ruined. "Tell me," said Prince Charming. "The matter is my misfortune rather than yours, yet I wept only one day, while you are still weeping. Why should that be so?"

"Oh, my Prince," sobbed the *bach mameluke*. "If you wept for a whole day after seeing yourself for only a minute, how long ought I to weep? I have gazed on you every day since you were born, and shall do till I die!"

Let me end this letter by telling you of a laugh or two we owed to Alexandre. His fall, during the polka, had irritated him a little, and when he is piqued he has a sarcastic turn of wit. In every country in the world, Madame, even in Tunis, some women are confirmed wallflowers while others dance all night. At this ball were two sisters, each married to an important Tunisian merchant, both of them perfect models of Moorish beauty, one weighing probably two hundred pounds and the other two hundred fifty. They had been sitting out for some time, and Laporte, anxious that all his guests should enjoy themselves, sought out Alexandre and begged him to invite one of them to dance the next quadrille, while Laporte himself would invite the other. Alexandre agreed somewhat reluctantly. "Which lady will you choose?" inquired Laporte. "The one there's least of!" my graceless son replied.

A little later M. Rousseau tried to interest him in a charming young girl who held herself somewhat aloof from the general gaiety, with an air of dignity and sadness that was really most becoming. "Yes," said Alexandre in reply to Rousseau's whispered praises, "I agree she's good looking, distinguished, too, if you like that style. What about her?" "Her father has been sent to the galleys!" "Well! Well! Why ever didn't they invite him to the ball? He wouldn't have been able to come, I suppose, but the conventions would have been satisfied, which might have cheered her up!" (They might indeed have invited him, for he was an honorable man, merely suspected of being concerned in an ancient and almost forgotten conspiracy against His Highness the Bey.)

Tomorrow at four o'clock your friends, Madame, are invited to a ceremonial dinner given in their honor by the consuls of each of the twelve powers represented in Tunis, and by all the European merchants of the town. The only consul whose presence we shall not enjoy is the Englishman, Sir Thomas Ride, who was one of Napoleon's jailers on Saint Helena. His manner is very distant and reserved. Either he ignores his colleagues or is ignored by them, probably the latter in my opinion.

In the evening there will be a grand ball in our honor at the consulate of Sardinia. I'll wager you would never have believed, Madame, that dancing was so popular in Tunis!

15

⚜ ⚜ ⚜

FAREWELL TO TUNIS

We spent six days in Tunis, Madame, and the time flashed past like an hour. I can scarcely do more than touch upon a few of the many curious things we saw and heard there, that still remain to be told.

On our first visit to the bazaar we forgot to look at the stall where gold dust is sold, and went back later to repair this omission. The vendor told us how he and his colleagues obtain this precious powder, which is the chief basis of trading between the tribes of the interior. It is to be found in certain spots in the desert south of Touggourt, but is invisible by daylight, for while the sun is shining the gold-bearing sand cannot be distinguished from ordinary sand. At night it shines with a phosphorescent glow, but, unfortunately for those who would gather it, as darkness falls, scorpions and horned vipers come out of their holes in such numbers that, to quote our friend the gold dust merchant, the furrows they make in the sand look like fishermen's nets. The ingenious gold-seekers overcome these difficulties by covering their camels' feet and legs with leather boots, too thick for poison fangs to pierce, and riding into the desert by night, carrying bags of coal dust. Wherever the sand is phosphorescent they outline the area thickly with black dust, so that at daybreak, when the deadly snakes have vanished, they can go back and gather their harvest.

Another stall in the bazaar offered me a fine lion skin, but

137

the price was out of all reason. The trader, who had bought it from a hunter, was able to tell me that it had been killed in the mountains around Constantine, an area that immediately made me think of our famous French lion-killer, Gérard.[1] To my delight the Arab knew him at once, and went on to assure me, with the poetic exaggeration natural to his race, that by now Gérard has killed at least a thousand lions, and no longer bothers with lionesses!

The chief subject of conversation in Arab tents is the lion, whom they call *Sid*, which means "Lord," and they believe that in the first three months of the year he slays demons; in the second three months he eats human flesh, in the third, nothing but a special clay; and in the fourth, animals. The Arabs have noticed that though a lion can carry off a bull, a horse, or even a camel, he has the greatest difficulty in coping with a sheep, and they believe this is because he forgot to ask Allah's aid, assuming that he would be able to cope with such a small animal unassisted. They believe that the lion can understand human speech in all languages, and when they hunt him they are careful to bear this in mind. The first man who catches sight of him lying concealed in some thicket points with his finger and shouts: *"Rahe-hena,"* which means: "He is not there." (If he dared to shout *"Ra-hena,"* meaning "There he is," the lion would understand and would rush out to devour the man who had denounced him.) Then the hunters withdraw far enough to escape the first three bounds the lion will make, a total of some sixty yards, and hurl insults at him till he emerges from cover. Rarely does a lion hunt end without the loss of at least two or three hunters, for, even when a bullet has pierced his heart, a lion can still slaughter any foe he can reach. Yet, they think, a lion is terrified of women and will not attack one unless hunger has driven him to desperation. They credit the lion with all the noble virtues, chivalry, and the ability to recognize and spare any adversary whose courage

---

1. Jules Gérard (1817–1864), known as *"le tueur de lions,"* was an officer of the Spahis.—*Ed.*

is equal to his own. A coward he will slay and eat at leisure, leaving only the hands and feet.

From the bazaar we went on to the *Dar-el-Bey*, the Palace of the Bey, where the Duke of Montpensier stayed during his recent visit. I found that the staff there retained a vivid memory of his gracious manner and his generosity on leaving. There was nothing of special interest in the palace itself,[2] except some modern sculptures by Hadj'-Younis, the artist whose work I had seen and admired at the tomb of Saint Louis. Since I particularly wanted to have a characteristic Arab room in the house I am having built near Paris, I inquired for his address and sent Paul to bring him to me. An hour later Younis stood before me, a handsome man of forty or forty-four years, with fine black eyes and a straight nose, his beard a little gray at the tip, his dress casually elegant. With him came his son, aged about twelve, named Ahmed, whose beauty has since become celebrated throughout Paris.

I asked Younis if he would come to France with me. He replied that he was quite accustomed to traveling, having been to Mecca, and would very much like to see France, if his son could come too. I agreed with a gesture, and inquired: "What wages would you ask?" He reflected a moment, then asked: "Should we live in your house and be lodged and fed in the way we are used to?"

"You shall prepare your own meals," I assured him, "and arrange your room to suit yourselves."

"Would you pay me 400 piasters of my wages in advance, for me to leave with my wife?"

"Certainly."

"Then I ask four piasters a day for my services and two for my son's."

"No. That is not enough. I will pay you twice as much."

2. Here Dumas does less than justice to the Dar-el-Bey, which contains many rooms beautifully decorated in typical Moorish style of the eighteenth century. Its Judgment Hall has a domed roof adorned with the delicate arabesque plasterwork known as "Nursh Hadida."—*Ed.*

He gave me a searching glance and turned doubtfully toward Laporte, who understood his thought at once and replied: "You can trust his word. He will keep his promise."

"Are you, then, some great lord?" Hadj'-Younis asked in wonder.

"No, but I am a man who appreciates talent and likes to reward it."

"Then I am your man, provided the Bey will allow me to go with you."

"The deuce!" exclaimed Laporte. "I never thought of that."

In point of fact this might present a serious problem, for the Bey does not like his subjects to travel, in case they acquire a taste for emigration. Younis, too, was busy with sculpture ordered for the Bey's tomb. Clearly, I needed to discuss the matter with the Bey personally, so once more Laporte and I set out in his carriage for Bardo. Having heard such terrible stories about the place, I almost dreaded going there again and facing the formidable *Boabs*, but they bowed to us respectfully and ushered us into the Bey's presence. (It is much simpler to obtain an audience with the Bey than with a minor official of the French government.) He received us cordially, asking whether I had brought him more good news. Laporte explained that I had come to ask a favor of His Highness. "Then I shall have good news for him," said the Bey, but as Laporte went on to explain my request I watched his face darken a little as he replied: "But does your friend, the savant, know that Younis is working for me?"

"Yes, Your Highness," I returned, "but I am sure you will understand. For you, he is preparing your tomb. For me, I hope he will build a room that I can use while I am still living. Your need is naturally less urgent than mine." My reply struck the Bey as a piece of sound reasoning, and after reflecting for a few moments he went on: "Very well. I will let you have Hadj'-Younis. Treat him kindly and send him back to me as soon as you can." I thanked the Bey with much more heartfelt gratitude than when he promised me the Order of Nisham!

So Younis' passport was signed and handed to us before we left, and when we returned to the consulate the sight of this document gave even more joy to the sculptor than it had to me. He was manifestly excited at the prospect of coming to France, and Paul, as I learned later, had given him an enthusiastic account of the comforts he would enjoy in my home. I may add that I have scrupulously honored my obligation toward him, and in a letter Younis wrote to his wife after spending four months with me he expressed his satisfaction in the picturesque phrase: "We are living like mice in a cheese."

I must say a word or two about the College of Saint Louis, whose principal, while we were there, was M. Espinasse. When the tomb I told you of was built, a worthy churchman, Abbé Bourgade, was sent to conduct services in the adjoining chapel. In his leisure moments he dreamed of extending this foothold of Western civilization in Africa, and, on his request, fifteen sisters of charity of the Order of Saint Joseph were sent from France to help him. These devout women succeeded in founding a sanctuary, a girls' school and a hospital in memory of Saint Louis. The abbé's next project was a College for Boys, which he managed to establish when the King of France sent him 1,000 francs, a gift that later became an annual donation. Now, the college has more than two hundred students who are equally conversant with French, Italian and Arabic, their studies covering a wide range of subjects, including chemistry, physics and line-drawing. Our visit caused a certain excitement there, and four or five boys were chosen to show us round. On a blackboard I saw lines of Arabic symbols that the class translated for my benefit, a series of proverbs and maxims, some of which struck me as interesting: "The word that escapes your lips is your master"; "Patience is the key to happiness; haste leads only to repentance"; "A sensitive soul is always in mourning"; "Who strikes a dog, strikes its master"; "Though your friend be sweet as honey, do not lick him away!"

On leaving the college we came across Giraud, torn be-

141

tween laughter and disappointment. He and Boulanger had noticed a charming Moorish figure, young and lissome, and, encouraged as they thought by her flashing eyes smiling through the folds of her *haik*, they followed her. She spoke no French, they knew no Arabic, so they were reduced to conversing as best they could in the primitive tongue of the ancient Celts,[3] and it was some time before they realized that their beautiful Moor was not a girl, but a boy! In this land it is very difficult to recognize girls from boys at first glance, for they have the same beauty of movement, the same shining dark eyes, red lips and pearly teeth, and wear the same enveloping draperies that hide more than they reveal.

We had put off our final purchases until the last possible moment, but as we returned to the consulate about two o'clock the bazaar was open and we could no longer escape. Imagine how strongly, yet how ineffectually, Madame, I wrestled against the temptations of gold necklaces, bracelets and brooches; the finest silks and gauzes woven with broad bands of gold thread; carpets from Smyrna or Tripoli; little mother-of-pearl tables. At every fresh place I visit, my luggage is increased by three or four large packing cases!

We reached the consulate to find Younis and his son waiting for us, each carrying a little parcel with a change of clothing, and their tools rolled up in a cloak. Outwardly they were as calm as though they were merely going to Goletta, kissed my hand in greeting, addressed me as *Sid*, "master," and confidently left it to me to take care of them in every way, protecting them from the unknown dangers they felt must surely exist on such a journey. They brought two fowls with them, in case we ran short of food tomorrow, and all Paul's eloquence failed to convince them that their birds were completely unnecessary.

So the moment came for us to leave our friends Laporte,

3. "Celt" is the generic name of an ancient people who inhabited parts of central and western Europe in pre-Roman times and later spread to North Africa and Asia Minor. Their language had certain roots which persisted in Breton, Welsh, Cornish, Erse and Gaelic.—*Ed.*

Rousseau, our other compatriots who had given us such a fine banquet, and Sainte-Marie, who was just about to set out on another hazardous expedition. Fifty came down with us to the shore, while from the terrace the ladies waved good-by. Night was falling rapidly and we had no time to lose, for the moon would not rise before midnight, so we exchanged our last embraces and jumped into the waiting boats. The posts marking the channel are almost impossible to see at night, and after an hour's rowing we realized we were lost on the lake, but eventually we managed to reach Goletta just as Monsieur Gaspari appeared on the jetty with a torch. We had to go ashore, for he had prepared a special punch for us, a flaming bowl concocted of bottles of *rosolio*, maraschino and two or three other liqueurs I had never heard of. Then he pressed me to accept the spoils of his research over the past ten years: medals, fragments of mosaic, the relics of various statues— one more packing case to add to the others.

At last, remembering that the *Véloce* was waiting for us with some impatience, we tore ourselves away from Goletta, as we had from Tunis, and at ten o'clock we were on board, enjoying a very welcome supper while the crew made ready to sail. At midnight a splendid moon rose and gave us our last glimpse of the Lake of Tunis, before we rounded Cape Carthage.

16

GALITA. BONA. STORA

With a calm sea and a good wind we made a steady seven knots all night, and at daybreak on December 10 found ourselves in sight of Galita, a little island something like Monte-Cristo, inhabited only by goats and rabbits. The idea of a couple of hours' shooting appealed to us, the Captain readily agreed, so the *Véloce* dropped anchor a gunshot's length from shore in seventeen fathoms of water with a bottom of thick clay and seaweed. It was not possible to bring her closer in, for the shallows bristled with sharp-pointed rocks fallen from the cliffs above, so the ship's boat was launched and we were rowed toward the shore, meeting on the way a small craft manned by some Neapolitan coral-fishers with whom we exchanged a word or two.

We found some difficulty in reaching land, and were at last compelled to leave the boat, climb on a rock, and jump from one pinnacle to the next until we could set foot on the beach. There, to our disappointment, the going was equally rough, but we pressed on over a formless chaos of boulders until we gained a flat stretch of pebbles where sparse grasses grew to a height of two feet. Almost at once a couple of rabbits darted away in front of me and by good luck I bagged them both. As the sound of the shots echoed from the cliffs we saw a herd of wild goats bounding to the summit of the crags on our right, and Alexandre, Desbarolles and the young ship's doctor at once set out in pursuit, a dangerous move, as it seemed to

144

me, in view of all these loose rocks ready to roll into the sea at a touch. However, as I might have expected, my words of caution were repulsed and overruled. Maquet, Giraud, Chancel and I were left behind to continue beating the lower ground to the left, where we found good sport with the rabbits, shooting twenty or so, while Chancel also brought down a woodcock.

Occasionally we heard an answering shot from the mountain, and once, as I looked up, I saw Desbarolles sliding rapidly down the side of a rock, not in either of the positions favored by the devotees of Sidi-Fathallah, but on his posterior, to the serious detriment of his trousers and underpants, as we learned later. Alexandre, too, met with what could have been a nasty mishap. After running down a slope he could not stop himself; his legs looked like a pair of compasses stretching from rock to rock, and he managed to save himself only by thrusting the butt of his gun between two boulders which halted his headlong strides, though the butt itself broke under the strain. Fortunately these were the only accidents of the day.

I need hardly add that they failed to add a goat to our spoils. Every hunter had done his best and had fired countless shots without bringing down a single one, so we concluded that the goats of Galita must be invulnerable, or at least vulnerable, like Achilles, only in the heel, and the heel of a goat, Madame, is a target any marksman might miss. Alexandre's skill, at any rate, was beyond question, for he tossed a pebble into the air and pulverized it with his last bullet.

Back on the shore, we found the sailors had rounded up a few rabbits for themselves while waiting, among them a white one that its compatriots seemed to regard with profound astonishment. One man, exploring a kind of quarry, had discovered a fine spring of sparkling ice-cold water where others before us had slaked their thirst, for the quartermaster of a French crew had carved a word of thanks on the rock that overhung it. So we made our way back on board, and the *Véloce* set sail again, running along the coast till, at midnight, she dropped anchor in the port of Bona.

145

The two things that first struck us when we went on deck were the Casbah, or fortress, the scene of one of Yusuf's earliest and most daring coups,[1] and the Lion Rock, a promontory we were destined to know more about that same evening. Sailors think very little of the harbor of Bona, where an anchor cannot take firm hold of the shifting sand, and never take refuge there unless forced by some sudden emergency. Forty years ago Bona was a rich town with a population of ten thousand, but in 1830, at the time of the French conquest of Algeria, it housed no more than fifteen hundred, for the productive wheat lands of the Crimea killed the export of grain from Africa, where, instead of wresting from their soil that rich superfluity which is the basis of commerce, men were reduced to growing simply what they could eat themselves.

Word of our voyage had spread along the coast, and scarcely had we dropped anchor when we saw a boat leave the shore and make for the *Véloce*. It brought the French Commissioner, an old friend of mine, come to kidnap us, so he said, and take us to his home where his wife and daughter were waiting to greet us. Later we took a few short walks in the town itself, but found nothing very interesting except a rather lovely mosque and a "miraculous" Bible in the Jewish synagogue, though why it was called "miraculous" no one could tell me. We decided upon an outing to Hippo, where St. Augustine lived as bishop for more than thirty years, your favorite author, Madame, whose *Confessions* you rightly prefer to those of Rousseau. Our host offered to provide horses for us, but the distance was only a mile or two and, for my part, I preferred to walk, with my gun over my shoulder, hoping for the chance of a shot or two and enjoying the company of a Polish colonel who had offered to guide me to the general rendezvous, the tomb of St. Augustine.

1. Bona was occupied by the French for a few months in 1830, and reoccupied in 1832, when Captain Yusuf, with Captain Armandy and a small force of marines, seized the Casbah and held it till the arrival of reinforcements.

On leaving the town we crossed a great marsh stretching to the sea on our left and the mountains on our right. Ahead of us the horizon was bounded by a range of hills, on whose lower slopes the sacred tomb was built. We followed the right bank of the Seybuse, where I killed a few snipe and a wild duck before rejoining the rest of our party at the tomb. It is built on the ruins of the ancient city of Hippo Regius, the residence of the Numidian kings, but nothing of them remains, not even their names, so completely has the mantle of St. Augustine covered everything for which the town is remembered. He is the saint that women worship, the saint of poetry and love, who struggled all his life against the burning desires of his own heart, who first made conjugal love his ruling passion and then made a cult of filial devotion. He was born at Tagaste on the 13th of November, 354, and was brought up at Madaura. He visited Carthage and was disgusted by its dissolute ways, for nothing is further from debauchery than love; Milan, where the eloquence of Bishop Ambrose led to his conversion; and finally Hippo, where he became bishop in 395. He died on August 22, 430, during the third siege of Hippo by the Vandals, and though they destroyed the town they respected the bishop's palace and his library, the saint's only possessions, which he left to the Church. His body was claimed by Cagliari, then by Pavia. At last, in 1842, the French government claimed a part of the precious relics for the new Hippo, and the saint's right forearm was placed on board the *Gassendi*, taken to Hippo and buried with great pomp at the spot where the monument stands today. By a singular coincidence it was Captain Bérard, now of the *Véloce*, who was in command of the *Gassendi* at that time.

Of the monument itself I will say nothing. Was it lack of money or of skill that made it so unworthy of the saint? Let us hope it was lack of money. The pilgrim to the shrine had best turn his back on it and feast his eyes on the magnificent view, the ruins of the old town in the foreground, in the middle distance the marshes bisected by the Seybuse, and beyond them the amphitheater of the town lying with the mountains to the left, and to the right the sea.

My friends and I held a council there on a point of some importance to us. Should we go direct from Bona to Constantine via Guelma, or should we take the usual route through Stora and Philippeville? The road through Guelma was more difficult, but more picturesque, and it was in that place that I had long been expecting to meet Gérard the Lion-killer, so we were all inclined to choose that route until the Polish officer took from his pocket a letter addressed to me by Gérard himself. It was dated two days earlier and informed me that he was just leaving for the interior to kill a lioness and her two cubs that were terrorizing an Arab village.[2] Guelma's chief attraction for us was Gérard, and on hearing of his absence we naturally decided to take the road via Philippeville.

On our return from Hippo we found an excellent dinner awaiting us at Bona, followed by an evening party that was typically French. Our host's daughter sang the latest songs for us, and played some of the most delicately intricate piano music of Monpou, Thalberg, Dreychock and Liszt. Albums were opened for our entertainment, and in response we each added something to their pages. Giraud drew a caricature, Boulanger a portrait, Alexandre, Maquet and I managed some verses, while Desbarolles ventured on a quatrain. We could have believed ourselves in a drawing room in the Chaussée-d'Antin, especially since, outside, the rain was pouring down.

The storm caused us some anxiety, for I knew that the harbor of Bona was reputed to be treacherous. Our host did his utmost to persuade us to stay overnight. The weather was frightful. Why not enjoy shelter and good companionship for a few hours longer? What did it matter whether we left tonight or in the morning? But I noticed that Commandant Bérard looked grave at this suggestion, and though, had I

2. In the original, Dumas gives circumstantial accounts of nine of Gérard's lion hunts, based on information given him by the hunter himself, when they met later in Paris. Dumas used some of this material again in his *Causeries* (1860).

seemed disposed to fall in with it, I know he would have agreed at once, pending my decision he stood cap in hand, ready to leave. So we explained that since we must be in Algiers by the 20th at the latest, and still had to visit Philippeville and Constantine, every hour was precious. Besides, we much preferred to travel at night, so that all our waking hours could be filled with sight-seeing. The good-bys that began in the drawing room were continued all the way to the quay, for our host and all the gentlemen of the party insisted on escorting us there with every umbrella they could muster.

The sea was very rough, even in the harbor. A sickly moon peered fitfully through a yellowish haze, while over half the sky a great black cloud, fantastically shaped like a two-headed eagle, hung motionless. When we reached the *Véloce* we found that the men aboard her fully expected we should spend the night ashore and had made no preparations for getting under way. Even the boilers were cold, but the moment he stepped on deck Commandant Bérard gave his orders and instantly every man set to work. By now the weather seemed to have improved somewhat, and the night was clear enough for us to see the outline of the gigantic Lion Rock. Except for the bilious moon and the strange black cloud, which Vial alone persisted in distrusting, there seemed nothing to cause alarm, and half an hour later we had weighed anchor and set sail. Immediately, as though the elements had been waiting to catch us at their mercy, the wind, which had died down for a while, freshened again to gale force and the great cloud broke in such torrential rain that my friends and I were driven below. We took refuge in the officers' quarters where we had spent so many convivial hours with our friends Vial, Salles and Maquet that we felt very much at home. At present we had the place to ourselves, for every man was on duty.

We were still in party mood—the effect of tea, piano music and albums—and none of us felt inclined to go to bed except Maquet, who, as usual, lay down as soon as the ship began to move, but left his cabin door open so that he could continue to enjoy our company, as far as a man expecting to be seasick could enjoy anything. Giraud began to rough out a sketch he had had in mind for some time, of Maquet knocking his head against a low doorway; Alexandre was busy, trying to improve on the verses he had inscribed in our hostess' album an hour or two earlier; and I settled down to write a letter to the Duke of Montpensier to thank him for the Order of a Commander of Charles III, which he had sent to me at Algiers as a gift to commemorate his wedding. Soon we were all engrossed in our various activities, quite oblivious of the wind and rain outside, scarcely aware that the ship was rolling much more than usual.

Suddenly, above the noise of the storm, we heard the Captain shout: "Hard aport!" and the helmsman reply: "She's over as far as she'll go, sir!" Another voice yelled, with an oath to split the heavens: "We're on the Lion!" and we all instantly rushed up on deck. You cannot imagine, Madame, the sight that met our eyes. A flash of lightning, ripping through a curtain of rain like a dense volley of arrows, showed us we were barely ten yards from the Lion Rock, our bow, covered with foam, almost touching the boulders at its base. "Full astern!" cried the Captain in a voice that rang through the ship. At once the engines were thrown into reverse and the *Véloce* shuddered at the sudden check, but still crept forward a few seconds longer. "Eight fathoms," shouted the sailor heaving the lead. "Six—five fathoms." But now the ship hung motionless. Once more the Captain ordered "Full astern!" and this time, after a moment of agonizing uncertainty, the paddle wheels churned the water and began to pull us back from the jaws of death. It was a very near thing, Madame. Had those wheels turned forward only twice more, we should have split open on those fearful rocks, and in all probability you would have had a most devoted servant in the next world.

Soon we were in deep water again. "Let go the port anchor," shouted Bérard, and we heard it splash overboard, its chain rattling across the deck with a fearful din, but the chain proved too short to allow the vessel room enough to swing in safety, and the anchor had to be abandoned. In the midst of all these maneuvers the *Véloce* had fired two or three guns to warn the harbor master at Bona that a ship was in peril, but, ten minutes later, we managed to regain our former berth without help from the shore, our starboard anchor holding firm in seventeen fathoms, in spite of the slimy bottom. My friends and I had long since gone below again, for the wind and rain made it impossible for us to stay on deck. Indeed, our presence there was a hindrance to the crew, so we wandered back to the wardroom, where, fatuously enough, we tried to interest ourselves in our interrupted sketches, verses and letter-writing. When, a little later, Vial came down, bruised and battered by the storm, drenched to his very bones, he found us looking as calm as though we were still in the *salon* at Bona. "Good God!" he exclaimed. "Don't you realize, my lads, that the Lion very nearly swallowed us?" "Yes. We know," we replied, imperturbable as Spartans, and Vial stared at us in amazement.

We were out of danger but still in considerable discomfort, for the ship was rolling so much that we had to lie down. Chairs and stools were staggering wildly across every open space. Every time we rolled to port another bullet fell out of a bag left lying open on a shelf and joined its fellows as they rattled to and fro across the cabin floor, in unison with a cannon ball rolling on the deck above. Maquet was no longer suffering alone. Giraud, too, was prostrate, while Desbarolles wandered up and down between the tottering chairs like a soul in torment, clutching his head and repeating over and over again: "This is amazing! . . . I feel seasick! . . . Me! . . . Astonishing!" We had no rest until five in the morning, when the sea began to moderate a little, the furniture stopped reeling and the bullets settled in a corner. Desbarolles held his head in both hands, like Marius at the ruins of Carthage, and we all fell asleep at last.

But not for long. Soon after daybreak we were on deck again, looking at Bona through a curtain of fine rain. The ship was still rolling in the strong swell from the North, and the Captain decided to move to an anchorage near Fort Gênois, which offered much better shelter than Bona, as we found when we reached it at nine in the morning. The weather was still overcast, blowing a gale from the west, and we watched great waves breaking right over the Cape of la Garde with clouds of spray more than a hundred feet high. Further out the sea was mountainous, but in any case Commandant Bérard had no intention of leaving the area without recovering his lost anchor, so the crew had their work cut out for that day and probably for the next as well.

We lay about six hundred yards off shore, opposite a mountain covered with scrub, and Maquet, exhausted by *mal de mer*, begged to go hunting there with the doctor, so the Captain had a boat launched to take them in. We watched them go off happily into the woods, where, as we learned when they came back at five o'clock, they enjoyed a good day's sport stalking two hyenas, without, however, managing to come up with them. I stayed on board to finish my letter to the Duke of Montpensier; Giraud rested in Vial's airy deck cabin; Desbarolles and Boulanger fell fast asleep on a bench, their faces caressed by a sunbeam that broke through the clouds; while Alexandre and Chancel settled down to a game of cards. My two Arab protégés came on deck to enjoy a smoke. During the uproar of the night they were fully convinced that their last hour had come, but with true Moslem fatalism had quietly awaited whatever Allah willed. The crew had been given time off duty to make up for their sleepless night, and were lying around between decks. So, for all on board, the day passed in very welcome peace and quiet. At dinner that evening all the conversation naturally turned on our escape, even the officers agreeing that it had been a very close shave. No one felt inclined to stay up late, so as soon as the meal was over we parted for the night, and by ten o'clock we were all sleeping soundly.

During the night the wind dropped and the sea grew calmer, so in the morning the *Véloce* set out to search for her missing anchor, and lay to about five hundred yards from the Lion Rock. We landlubbers were completely mystified as to how anyone could find an anchor lost at the bottom of the bay, but the sailors seemed to think it the simplest thing in the world. I very much hoped they were right, for we had already lost three days. Commandant Bérard had already sent to Bona for lighters—barges shaped something like our river ferryboats but larger—and while waiting for them one of our men dived again and again to look for the anchor. At the fourth or fifth attempt he found it lying in forty-five feet of water. The next task was to take down a cable and thread it through the ring of the anchor. This took longer, but after half a dozen fruitless efforts the sailor surfaced with the cable end in his hand and announced that the job was now as good as done.

By this time the barges had drawn alongside, and with their help we began the operation of hauling up the anchor from the muddy bottom, very hard work that kept all hands toiling at the capstan. I have not, I think, mentioned to you, Madame, that in Bona I came across a poor family of traveling musicians from Malta, who had exhausted the demand for their services in that part of Africa and begged for a passage to Algiers. Commandant Bérard agreed to take them there at my request, and between us we collected enough money to provide them with food for the journey, so that they would be no expense to the *Véloce*. Ever since they came aboard we had completely forgotten the poor devils, but now we suddenly saw them coming up on deck with their instruments to give the men a tune to lighten their Herculean labors. No double ration of wine or issue of rum, not even a promise of extra pay, can cheer a sailor as music does, and the jaunty rhythm of Maltese polkas kept hands and feet working together to such good purpose that two hours later our anchor was back on board again and safely stowed.

That night we sailed further along the coast and next day anchored off Stora, the worst harbor in the world, next to

Bona. Even in the comparatively sheltered anchorage the sea was so rough that we had the greatest difficulty in getting off the *Véloce*. We planned to visit Constantine, and the Maltese musicians begged to come with us as far as Philippeville, where they thought they might give a concert. Consequently two boats instead of one had to be launched to take us and our luggage ashore. The waves were so high that sometimes these boats rose level with the deck and sometimes rolled in a trough ten feet below the bottom rung of the starboard ladder. Only by taking quick advantage of an occasional lull when boat and ladder converged did we contrive to slip down like beads from a broken necklace.

Remember that this was during comparatively calm weather, Madame. You cannot imagine what the waves are like at Stora during a tempest. On January 26, 1841, the corvette *La Marne* was wrecked in the harbor, and at the moment when she began to founder a great wave threw a Tuscan schooner clean over her. It passed between the mizzen and mainmast without even touching, and went on to bury its bowsprit part way up the cliff. This is no fable. The Captain of the *La Marne* gave a full account in his official despatch to the *Ministre de la Marine*, and the records of M. de Marqué, Commandant of the port of Stora, show that of the thirty-one ships sheltering in the harbor that day, only three cargo boats remained afloat after that disastrous storm. What do you think, Madame, of waves that can make ships play leapfrog?

❧   ❧   ❧

17

PHILIPPEVILLE. CONSTANTINE

You remember how difficult we found it to climb down from the *Véloce* into the boats? It was just as much of a problem to get from the boats to the quay, but having learned how to make the most of a momentary lull we managed to jump ashore safely. Never go to Stora, Madame! Once there, your only desire, as it was ours, would be to leave again as quickly as possible. Its houses? Eight or ten only, built on rising ground. Its streets? Merely a few slippery slopes and muddy flights of steps. Horses? A carriage? Any means of transport to take you on to Philippeville? Quite out of the question!

We hired a handcart and piled our luggage on it. Our Maltese friends insisted on pulling it as a practical expression of their gratitude, the rest of us shouldered our guns, and we started on our five-mile walk to Philippeville through a gentle shower of fine rain. The road itself was pleasant enough, winding up and down as all mountain tracks do, giving us a thousand unexpected views of the countryside or the open sea. Philippeville, as its name indicates, is a modern place. Not one mosque or minaret, no *marabouts* or palm-shaded fountains. Instead, it has uninteresting little houses like those in some suburb of Paris, inns with signs over their doors, billiard saloons displaying three balls, red, blue, white, and a pair of crossed cues.

We halted at the first hotel we came to. It was called the

Regency, and its prices for dinner and bed were so fantastically high that we at once resolved to make sure of leaving next morning. Coaches run regularly from Philippeville to Constantine, but since we were unlikely to find one with eight vacant seats it was simpler to hire a conveyance for ourselves, and for very little more than the Regency charged us for one night we acquired the services of a coachman, five horses and a sort of omnibus for six days.

Philippeville is neither a village nor a town, but simply one long street that climbs for five hundred yards and then runs downhill for a further five hundred. The rising ground, open to the shore and the sea breezes, is a healthy place to live, but people with homes on the downward slope, facing inland, are, I was told, subject to long, slow fevers, very difficult to cure.

As we drove out of Philippeville, a magnificent landscape unfolded before our eyes, bounded on the horizon by mountains of wonderful shapes and colors. To left and right of the road, the fertile plains were thickly overgrown with tall esparto grass and prolific plants like irises, shooting up from bulbs sometimes as big as a man's head. In the flowering season the whole countryside must look like a carpet of blossoms. We met carts driven by countrymen wearing smocks, and passed uniformed roadmenders working on the highway. We could well have imagined ourselves still in France, except that every now and again we caught sight of an Arab shepherd in the shade of a little wood, his eyes sparkling fiercely beneath the hood of his tattered burnoose, his traditional crook as proudly borne as a scepter in the hands of an emperor. A hundred yards further on we would see a tent covered with black and white sheepskins like the tents of the Ishmaelites in the Bible, with thorn bushes in a circle around it to keep off jackals and hyenas.

About five o'clock we arrived at El-al-Rouch, which our soldiers call *la Rousse*. It is not only a village but a camp as well, and the first houses one comes to are fortified with turrets. They command a kind of protective earthwork that

156

successfully resisted a long seige by the Arabs, though it would not have survived an attack by regular troops for an hour. We halted at a ramshackle hotel built of rough planks, and were conducted up a kind of ladder, every rung creaking under our feet, to a long narrow room like a passage. It held two beds, a third was hastily added, and Alexandre, the doctor and I instantly claimed all three. Where our other friends were to sleep I neither knew nor dared to inquire, but in any case they could not have been worse off than we were, for cold winds blew fiercely in upon us, not only through the doors and windows but through the walls, which were mere partitions, and up between the gaping floor boards too. Yet, I swear, I was conscious of a strange sense of well-being. I thought of you and our friends, the Théâtre Historique being built for me in Paris, where we were to present *La Reine Margot*. Why the devil should I be thinking of *La Reine Margot* in this lonely hut in Africa, open to all the winds of the desert and all the noises as well, for I assure you there was plenty of noise! The sentinels challenged every passer-by with "Who goes there?"; cocks were crowing, pigeons cooing, dogs barking, while slightly further away jackals yelped and hyenas howled all night.

We had arranged to leave at 7 A.M., but, as usual, we were late, and it was 8:30 when we started off. We had a long way to go, for we had made up our minds to reach Constantine before nightfall. About midday we stopped for lunch at Smindou, a combined farm and camp. On our return journey we should probably spend the night there, and I trembled in advance at the thought of where, and on what, we should sleep!

Paul, who had become slow and torpid with the cold, as serpents do, traveled on the box beside our driver, a charming and most obliging man. A few miles out of Smindou, Paul, swaddled in his cloak, rolled like a ball from the driver's seat to the shaft and thence to the ground, picked himself up unhurt, came to the carriage door and in his blandest voice inquired: "This is the place where carriages usually upset.

Would the gentlemen prefer to dismount or remain seated?"
We all got out, deciding to take our guns in the hope of a
little sport, and arranging to rejoin our carriage a few miles
further on, at a place where the road made an elbow bend.

I do not know whether the Mistral, which Méry hates so
much, can compare in violence with the wind that blows in
the region around Constantine, but I do know that there were
times when we were literally brought to a standstill. Hunting was impossible in such a gale. Partridges that rose in front
of us flew into the wind and shot out of sight like bullets,
though I did manage to bring one down. A magnificent vulture circled overhead, probably out of range, for my shot
did not disturb him in the least. We pressed on against the
wind, and against a storm of fine hail that pricked our faces
like needles. Fortunately we found shelter in a village where
we managed to buy some bread, wine and eggs, and when
our driver pulled up at the same café for his customary bottle
we regained possession of our conveyance.

About four o'clock we reached a charming little place, half
French, half Arab, sheltered by palm trees and weeping wil-
lows, and called La Hamma. Its charm was deceptive, for it
owed its attractive verdure to its position in the middle of
a swamp, and I was told that the death rate there was un-
usually high. I particularly wished to stay there long enough
to sketch the village, but our driver assured us that if we
went on we should see something much more interesting in
half an hour, whereas, if we delayed at La Hamma, we should
pass a wonderful view after nightfall, and so should see nothing of it. Accordingly, threatening him with the full weight
of our annoyance if his promised view fell short of his description, we started off again at a rapid trot. Thirty minutes
later we rounded a mountain side, and as our carriage halted
a cry of admiration, almost of terror, broke simultaneously
from us all. Beyond a somber gorge, on the crest of a great
cliff bathed in the last red rays of the setting sun, there lay
before our incredulous eyes a town as fantastic as Gulliver's
Flying Island.

As we stood speechless with amazement and awe before this phenomenon, a man on a fine Arab horse galloped up to us. He was a Pole, employed by the Palais Royal, one of the best in Constantine. Somehow he had learned that we were on our way to the town (How? Heaven knows! Perhaps the vulture I missed flew over to warn him!) and had ridden out to solicit our patronage for his hotel. We heartily consented, and since the road made a long detour he offered to guide us to the town by a footpath that would take us there in twenty minutes. He warmly invited us to use his horse, but it could hardly carry us all and we insisted on his remaining in the saddle. Besides, I doubted whether either of us could manage his high-bred mount as he did. It was marvelous to watch him leaping from rock to rock in the gathering dusk, balancing on the very brink of an abyss, scaling the steep mountain side and sending down an avalanche of small stones, sometimes wheeling to come back down and make sure we were following safely, all without a single false step, though the gradient was so steep that we poor footsloggers could scarcely keep upright. By now night had fallen thick and black; we sensed, but could not see, precipices all around us; and the hail had changed to an icy rain that stung our upturned faces, everything combining to impress on us the wild grandeur of the place and the fantastic unreality of our situation.

At last, after half an hour's climb, we came out on the high road ten minutes before our carriage was due, and walking on we soon passed under an archway like the entrance to a quarry. For ten paces we marched in utter darkness through one of Constantine's main gates, then suddenly saw the lights of the Palais Royal shining twenty yards ahead.

There a warm welcome awaited us, a good fire blazing and the landlord standing, candlestick in hand, to greet us. There was six inches of snow in the streets and on the roof tops, and knowing what little comfort there is in most Arab houses I fully expected to be as much too cold in Africa as I had been too hot in Italy. But I was wrong. Alexandre and I were conducted to a pretty little room where our host lit a fire for us as I glanced around, noticing to my disappointment that the four pictures on the wall were lithographs of popular French paintings. The muslin curtains dividing an alcove from the rest of the room had such an attractive design that I inquired whether I could buy some like them. The landlord replied that nothing could be simpler, especially in France, for the Arab traders imported them from Saint Quentin! More and more disillusioned I continued to look around the room, but the only item of African origin was the excellent carpet! For supper we ordered a cold chicken, and were served so promptly and well that I could hardly believe we were still in Africa. Alexandre offered to bet we had lost our way and were in Montmorency! Still, we spent a pleasant evening, Boulanger and Giraud with their sketchbooks, Chancel, Desbarolles, Maquet and I in bringing our notes up to date, while I also studied my *Salluste* in preparation for exploring Constantine next morning.

In the days of the Numidian kings, the name of the place was Cirta, and under Micispa,[1] who fortified the town, it mustered ten thousand cavalry and twenty thousand infantry. Having fallen into ruins, it was rebuilt early in the third century, A.D., by Constantine, who gave it its modern name in honor of his daughter Constancia. A century or so ago it was the capital of the four great provinces forming the Regency of Algiers, and was governed by a Bey. Its last six rulers reigned in quick succession between 1817 and 1837, for Beys seldom live long. The first of these, Mohamed-Bey, nicknamed Bou-Chattabiah, which means "Father of the Ax," was a madman with a lust for blood who was given that title because he used to behead with his own hands all criminals condemned to death. He kept his ax hanging at his doorway opposite the Café Turc, and on days when it had not tasted blood he used to pour over it a glass of wine or cup of coffee, to show he was keeping it in mind. Because of his stupid cruelty he was driven from the throne after a reign of one

1. Second century B.C.—*Ed.*

160

year and took refuge in Algiers, where he devoted himself to good works and died in the odor of sanctity in 1846.

Brahim-Bey-Gourbi succeeded him and reigned for a year before he was followed by Achmed-Bey, who took the throne for the second time and ruled for two years. Brahim-Bey-Gritti came to power in his turn, and was so beloved by his people that the Turks deposed him lest he should become too influential. Even then he could not escape the fatal destiny of the Beys of Constantine, for Achmed-Bey had him assassinated at Medea in 1834. His son is now an officer in the Spahis at Constantine. Mohammed-Bey-Monamany, who succeeded him, was a fine man, but was deposed because he did not collect taxes fast enough. Achmet, the last of the Beys, was a *koulougli*, the son of a Turk and a woman of the desert. After our conquest of Algeria he refused to recognize French authority, hence the expedition against Constantine in '36, which failed, and that of '37, which won the town for France, though at tragic cost.

One of the men who played an active and glorious part in that campaign was General Bedeau, Governor of Constantine at the time of our visit. I did not know him personally, but had heard so much about him from the Duke of Orléans that I had a high opinion of his qualities, and it was with considerable respect that I presented myself at Government House. The Governor had been informed of my arrival, and had heard as much about me from the Duke as I had heard about him, so we quickly improved our acquaintance in talking of our late friend whom we had both loved. Then the General ordered two officers of his General Staff, Boissonnet and Sade, to show me everything of interest in Constantine and the surrounding neighborhood. They were charming companions, aged between twenty-six and thirty, speaking Arabic like natives, and had studied Constantine as poets and philosophers as well as historians.

I will not attempt to describe the town to you, Madame. Mere words could not depict this network of streets, this tangle of Roman antiquities and modern reconstructions carried out since the French occupation, this eagle's nest perched on the summit of a crag. That is a task for the brush or pencil, not the pen. In the evening General Bedeau presented me to the chief citizens, the successors of the men who came before General Rulhières on the day when Constantine was captured, among them Ben Adjouz himself. One of the guests was a poet who not only knew my name but brought with him a scroll of his own verses written in my honor. Another guest was a Frenchman who from long habit had become more Arabic in his ways and costume than the Arabs themselves. He invited us all to ride with him on the morrow, and instantly General Bedeau promised to provide horses for us if we wished to go. My friends gladly accepted, but I preferred to remain in the General's library to learn all I could of Constantine and the peoples of this part of Africa, the Berbers, the Kabyles and Chaouias, Moors, Biskris and Negroes, the Arabs of the plains, the Touaregs, those dreaded pirates of the desert who prey on caravans and deal in slaves.

I read more tales than I can tell you here of the customs of these and many other tribes, their loves and hates, their rough justice and cruel vengeance, the subtle trickeries of wandering gypsies (for there are gypsies in Algeria as in Spain), the sensitive pride of honorable chiefs, the fierce skirmishes between Arab leaders and French troops. Here is a story of a different sort, which I hope will amuse you, Madame.

In Ferdj'Ouah lives a sheikh named Bou-Akas, a magnificent example of the typical Arab of the Eastern provinces, who still reigns over the territory conquered by his ancestors. After the French conquest he was persuaded to recognize the Governor of Constantine as being in authority over him, but though he has remained on peaceful terms he has never been prevailed on to visit the town in person, fearing to be taken prisoner. He pays a yearly tribute of 80,000 francs, and every autumn after harvest, on the same day at the same time his camels enter the same gate of Constantine bringing the exact sum, never a farthing short. He is forty-nine years old and wears the dress of the Kabyles, though he rules over twelve tribes.

One day he heard that the Cadi of one of his tribes was becoming famed for the wisdom of his judgment in matters of civil dispute, and wishing to form his own estimate of this new Solomon he set out incognito, like Haroun-al-Raschid. Wearing the dress of a merchant and riding a good Arab horse, he arrived at the town where the Cadi lived on a market day, and therefore a day when that chief would be sitting in judgment. Outside the gate a ragged cripple clutched at the horseman's burnoose and begged for alms. Like a good Moslem, Bou-Akas gave him money, but the beggar still clung to his benefactor, crying: "The Law does not say merely 'Give alms to thy brother,' but adds: 'Do all that thou canst to help him.'"

"Well," asked Bou-Akas, "what do you wish me to do for you?"

"Lord, I am, as you see, a poor cripple crawling on the ground like a serpent, and the streets are thronged. Save me from being crushed underfoot by mules and by camels, or by men! Take me up behind you and let me ride to the market place!"

"So be it," returned Bou-Akas, helping him up, though with some difficulty, and the ill-assorted pair rode on through the town. When they reached the market, the beggar pleaded: "Of your pity, Lord, dismount and help me down," but no sooner had Bou-Akas alighted than the rascal shouted: "Let go my horse's bridle!"

"What? You say my horse is yours?"

"Indeed he is mine! How dare you try to steal a cripple's only means of transport! Be off, stranger, or I will drag you before our Cadi. He is a just man, and will see at once that the horse must be mine, since because of my broken legs I cannot walk, while your limbs are strong and well able to carry you!"

"Ah!" said Bou-Akas to himself. "Here is my opportunity to test this Cadi's discernment." So he led his horse, with the beggar still perched on the saddle like a monkey, to the tribunal where justice was being administered in the open air, in the manner of the East. Two parties of litigants were already awaiting the Cadi's attention, so the Sheikh stood patiently till his turn should come, and listened with great interest.

The first case was a dispute between a *taleb* and a peasant. The writer claimed that the countryman had stolen his wife; the peasant insisted that she was not the writer's wife, but his own. The woman herself refused to say which man was her husband, but, being pressed for an answer, at last replied: "Neither or both," which made the affair most embarrassing. The judge pondered awhile, then said: "Leave the woman in my charge and come back tomorrow."

The second case concerned two shopkeepers, a butcher and an oil-seller, both covered with the stains of the goods they sold. Said the butcher: "I went to this man's shop to have my bottle filled with oil, but when I took a handful of money from my purse to pay him he seized my fist and cried that it was all his. So we have come here, I with the money in my hand, he with his hands around mine. By Mahomet I swear that this man lies when he says I stole his money. It is mine."

The oil merchant stated: "This man came to buy oil from me, and when I had filled his bottle he asked: 'Have you change of a gold piece?' I fumbled in my pouch and pulled out a handful of money which I placed on the sill of my shop to count, whereupon this butcher snatched it up and ran off with my oil and my money. So I seized his fist in both my hands and came to you, O Cadi, for justice. I swear by Mahomet that this man is lying when he says the money is his. It is mine."

The Cadi considered the matter and questioned each man in turn, but neither varied his story one iota. At last the judge said: "Leave the money here and come back tomorrow," so the butcher loosened his tight-fisted grip and placed the coins in a fold of the Cadi's mantle, whereupon both traders bowed low and went their different ways.

Now it was the turn of Bou-Akas and the legless cripple. The Sheikh explained to the Cadi exactly what had occurred; the rascal told such a plausible tale that he really sounded the rightful owner of the Arab steed. The judge made each repeat his evidence, heard them swear that it was true, and then ordered: "Leave the horse with me and come back tomorrow."

Next morning an interested crowd gathered at the tribunal, curious to hear how the Cadi would solve such difficult problems. He took the cases in the same order as before, and began by summoning the *taleb* and the countryman to his judgment seat. To the *taleb* he said: "Take away this woman, who is in truth your wife," and turning to his guards he commanded: "Take this peasant and punish him with fifty strokes on the soles of his feet."

After this sentence had been carried out in full view of the watching crowd, the Cadi called the shopkeepers to stand before him. To the butcher he said: "Here is your money, which you took from your own pocket as you testified. It was never in your accuser's possession. Take it, and go in peace. Guards! Give this oil-seller fifty strokes on the soles of his feet."

Now Bou-Akas and the beggar were called. "This is not so simple," said the Cadi. Turning to each of them he asked: "Could you pick out from twenty others the horse you say is yours?" Both assured him that they could. "Then come with me, one at a time. You first," continued the judge, and led Bou-Akas to his stable, where he at once recognized his horse. "Now go back to the tribunal, send your adversary to me here, and await my return." The beggar made his way to the stable as quickly as he could, and he, too, went straight to the horse he claimed as his own. "Very well," said the Cadi. "Follow me back to the place of judgment."

In the market place the judge resumed his seat and the

whole assembly waited impatiently for the return of the cripple, who because of his deformity could not keep up with
the rest. After five minutes he arrived, all out of breath, and
the Cadi pronounced his verdict. To Bou-Akas he said: "You
are the true owner of the horse. Go back to my stable and
claim it." Turning to the beggar he sentenced him to receive
fifty strokes on his posterior, prudently changing the site of
the punishment in view of the rascal's lack of feet.

When the Cadi returned home he found Bou-Akas waiting
for him, and inquired: "Are you, then, not satisfied with my
decision?" "Indeed, yes, but I desire to know what inspired
you in reaching your conclusions, which, I do not doubt,
were as correct in the other two cases as in my own. I am
not a merchant, but your ruler, Bou-Akas, Sheikh of Ferdj'-
Ouah, and I traveled here to find out for myself whether
your reputation as a just judge was well deserved." The Cadi
bowed to the ground and would have kissed his chief's hand,
but the Sheikh waved aside the ceremonious greeting. "Tell
me quickly. How did you know the woman was the *taleb*'s
wife? That the money belonged to the butcher, and that my
horse was really mine?"

"Lord, it is quite simple," replied the Cadi. "You remember
that I retained till the morning the woman, the money and
the horse?"

"Yes. I noticed that."

"At midnight I had the woman roused from a deep sleep
and ordered to clean my inkwell. She did so instantly and with
perfect skill. She had obviously performed the same task a
hundred times, so I said to myself: 'A peasant's wife would
not know how to clean an inkwell. She must be the wife of
the *taleb*.'"

"Of course! I see that!" the Sheikh replied, nodding his head
in agreement. "What about the money?"

"That was a different matter. Did you observe that the oil-
seller's clothes, and especially his hands, were slippery with
grease? Well, I placed the money in a vessel of clear water
and left it there all night. This morning I looked at it care-

fully, and there was not a single speck of oil floating on the water. If his story were true, the coins he took from his greasy pouch with his oily hands would have been covered with oil. Since there was no oil on them, they clearly must belong not to him but to the butcher."

"Good! Very true! Tell me how you knew the horse was mine."

"That was still more difficult, and even this morning I was in considerable doubt."

"Did that rascal pick out the right one from among twenty others?"

"Indeed he did, and was even more emphatic than you were. But my purpose in taking each of you, separately, to my stable was not to see whether you recognized the horse. It was to see whether he recognized you! When you went up to him he whinnied a welcome, but when the cripple came near him he kicked. So I said to myself: 'This horse must belong, after all, to the man who can walk, not to the cripple.' "

Bou-Akas pondered a moment, then replied: "The Lord is with you. You should be in my place, for you are worthy to be a sheikh, though I doubt whether I am wise enough to be a Cadi."

✤ ✤ ✤

18

MOORISH DANCERS. *The Camps at Smindoux and El-Arouch*

While I was reading and making notes in General Bedeau's library, Alexandre, Giraud, Desbarolles, Maquet and Chancel joined a riding party led by our compatriot Bonnemain, lieutenant of the local native regiment of Spahis, a French officer of the very best type, a man of the highest courage. He is a horseman of consummate skill, and gave my friends an exhibition they will never forget. He and his mount were as one, like a Centaur of old, and to entertain them he gave a demonstration of every maneuver known to the desert cavalry.

His parade ground was a small plateau bounded on one side by a precipice so sheer, so deep, that the River Rummel at its foot looked a mere thread of silver. A height to make a chamois giddy! Bonnemain rode his horse at full gallop toward this precipice, reined him in at the very brink, made him rear and turn a half-circle on his hind legs, his forelegs beating the empty air above the void like a compass tracing an imaginary arc in space. It was incredible! Sublime!

This escarpment, as I learned on their return, was the site of the ancient citadel, the Casbah, now used as a barracks and a store for ammunition. Great vultures with tawny bodies and white necks circle round these roofs like swallows, sometimes soaring till they look as small as larks, then dropping like a stone to within thirty or forty feet of the ground before spreading their wings again to sail slowly and majestically away. Why do vultures haunt this peak and no other? This is the crag (three times as high as the Tarpeian Rock in Rome), from which in former days unfaithful wives were thrown into the abyss, the vultures swooping down beside them to devour their shattered bodies on the rocky banks of the Rummel. This form of execution has now been abolished, but vultures still circle above this peak, hoping, like the Arabs, that French occupation will come to an end one day.

Our engineers have performed miracles at Constantine. I asked an Arab what he thought of these reservoirs, aqueducts, bridges, and he replied: "Mahomet must greatly love the Arab race, since he has brought men from beyond the sea to carry out for us this work that we could not do for ourselves." Like every other native of Constantine, he had the firm conviction that when our task was completed, God would send us home again. Algeria would no longer need us.

It is, perhaps, to be regretted that all these modern improvements have cost Constantine much of her former picturesque charm. She no longer has bazaars like those of Tunis. French uniforms throng her streets; her shops sell Indian calico and her traders speak Italian. To console me for this disappointment, my friends invited us to attend a Moorish ball. We hastened to accept, and can now appreciate the amazement of a certain Pasha of Algiers when he attended a reception at the home of a rich Neapolitan banker and saw his host waltzing. "If this man is indeed as rich as I have been told," he exclaimed, "why does he go to the trouble of dancing himself?" At a Moorish ball, Madame, the guests do not dance. They watch dancing girls.

We duly presented ourselves at nine that evening at a typical Moorish house, with the usual greasy lamp hanging from a hook in the wall to light a dilapidated stairway. The place seemed very poor until we reached the room where the dancers were waiting, the luxury of their dress all the more striking by contrast. Here, everything had been made ready for the occasion. The freshly whitewashed walls were almost dazzling in the light of lamps shaped like ostrich eggs; the floor was covered with that finely woven, delicately colored matting seen only in Arab countries, and seated upon it with their backs against a wall were three of four women, their legs bare to the knee, their slippers lying casually beside their feet. They wore velvet caps covered with gold sequins, velvet bodices, green or crimson satin pantaloons embroidered with gold thread, and while waiting they sat smoking cigarettes or drinking large cups of coffee.

Three of them were lovely girls between fourteen and eighteen years old; the fourth, still beautiful, might have been twenty-five. If their flesh lacked the firmness of marble, their skin was creamy and smooth; their arched brows met in a firm dark line over their voluptuous eyes, which sometimes gleamed as softly as black velvet, sometimes flashed like lightning. At the back of the room a series of steps had been arranged to accommodate the spectators, and in front of these steps a group of musicians, seated on the floor, were busy preparing their instruments, giving a tentative roll on their drums and rattling their tambourines. A side room, concealed by a simple curtain and lit by a single lamp, offered a certain degree of privacy to any who wished to discuss choreography with the dancers.

We went up to these ladies, who gave us their hands in greeting and offered us some of the cigarettes that they rolled with amazing dexterity. I was doing my best with smiles and gestures to open a conversation with the eldest dancing girl, when, with a blunt clarity that I found quite objectionable, she demanded champagne. "Huh?" said I, thinking I must have misunderstood. "Champagne!" repeated Fatima, with a gesture of raising a bottle to her lips, to assist my slow intelligence. Her meaning was only too obvious, so I took a few coins from my pocket and placed them in her hand, repeating the word with an intonation which meant: "For champagne, nothing more!" Fatima was quick to grasp my implication, and instantly shrugged her shoulders as though to say: "Get along! What do you take me for?"

For a moment I feared she might cause trouble, but I was

wrong. "Champagne" was the one and only French word Fatima knew. The ignorance of these poor creatures is almost beyond belief. When I questioned them through an interpreter, neither of the girls could tell me her age, though one of them leveled her hand at a certain distance from the floor and said: "My mother told me that is how tall I was when the French captured Constantine."

By now other spectators had arrived, officers from the garrison and two or three senior employees of the French administrative service. We were introduced to them and were pleasantly chatting when Fatima came back with a bottle in each hand, followed by a frightful-looking manservant carrying two more bottles. (These lackeys, hideous villains for the most part, are the indispensable personal attendants of all Moorish women living in towns.) The wine quickly vanished and seemed to put our dancers in the right mood, for one of them rose as slowly and gracefully as an adder, swayed for a moment like a young poplar in a breeze, then made a sign to the musicians and the dance began.

It was a strange dance, for the performer scarcely moved from the spot where she stood as the opening chords sounded. In each hand she carried an embroidered kerchief, her left hand covering her face while her right rested where modest Venus placed hers, but closer to the body. Her feet began to mark the rhythm, and as the tempo quickened her movements grew more and more voluptuous. She quivered and swayed, her outflung arms waved the kerchiefs in a graceful swirl of color, her lithe body bent forward and backward, slowly at first, then more and more swiftly until her sequined cap fell to the ground and her long hair swung like a curtain over her breast and shoulders or flew wide like a flag as she whirled. At last, when the dramatic tension seemed almost unbearable, the dance reached its climax in a wild cry of animal passion and the dancer sank fainting to the ground.

At once an older woman ran forward, raised the dancer in her arms and rubbed the end of her nose with the palm of her hand, whereupon the girl regained consciousness, rose to

171

her feet and began her dance again. Three times we watched the same sequence of events, the only variation being that by the end of her third performance certain other garments had followed her cap's example. Then the other dancers in turn entertained us with the same gyrations, the same cry of culmination, the same collapse and the same resurrection. No words can portray this dance to those who have not seen it, nor can the sketches that Boulanger and Giraud drew so industriously throughout the performance, for drawing cannot portray movement.

It was midnight when we left, very late for Constantine, where civilization has not yet reached the stage when dances go on until two in the morning. Here, the streets are as safe by night as by day, and, thanks to the firm rule of General Négrier, Constantine knows nothing of those street-corner hooligans who accost a pedestrian by night to inquire the time by his watch or help themselves to charity from his purse.

We left Constantine, and our kind host, General Bedeau, at two o'clock in the afternoon of December 22, in the same carriage that had brought us there. Our coachman, doubtless in a hurry to get home, no longer bothered to warn us of the places where coaches usually capsized, but though the vehicle frequently swayed alarmingly we arrived safely about six o'clock at the fortified camp of Smindoux where we were to pass the night.

There were only two solid habitations in the whole camp, a tiny stone-built house where the regimental Paymaster lived, and a wooden shack that served as an inn, which we entered. Having ordered supper, we tried to warm ourselves around a stove while waiting for our meal, but found it almost impossible because of the extreme humidity. Giraud and Boulanger went off to explore the upper floor in the hope of finding somewhere to sleep, but could find nothing better than a very drafty attic. They had just come back with this depressing report when our landlord came to me and inquired whether my name was Alexandre Dumas. On my affirmative reply he delivered a message from the Paymaster, presenting his compliments and placing at my disposal the ground floor of the little stone house which I had more than once glanced at with longing eyes.

I inquired whether there would be room enough for us all, and when I learned that it was a tiny place with only one bed I asked our host to convey my sincere thanks to the officer, regretting that I must decline. My friends, however, would not hear of my refusing this kind offer, protesting that there was no advantage in my sharing their discomfort. I was touched by their solicitude, but still felt most reluctant to deprive the Paymaster of his bed. The landlord replied that the officer had already prepared a camp bed for himself in the upper room. I should not cause him the slightest inconvenience. On the contrary, I should give him great pleasure, so I accepted, asking only to be allowed to thank him personally. The messenger did not respond to this suggestion, adding merely that the Paymaster had come home extremely tired and had already gone to bed. It would have been most inconsiderate to wake him up to thank him, so I did not insist, but followed my guide to the room where I was to spend the night.

It was a pretty little place with a pinewood floor, its walls hung with paper, everything in it fastidiously neat and clean. A fire was burning on the hearth, and as I stood by it I picked up a book from the mantelpiece, *Imitation of Jesus Christ*. On the flyleaf was written: "The gift of my very good friend, the Marquise of . . . ," but the name was scored out and illegible. I raised my head to look around, and my eyes rested on a little portrait of a woman of twenty-six or twenty-eight years, leaning on a window sill and gazing at the sky through prison bars. It was all so strange, so unexpected, that I seemed transported far from Africa and the camp of Smindoux. Even stranger was my conviction that the woman in the picture was someone I had once known. But when? Where? Who was she, and why was she in prison? How had our paths crossed? For an hour or more I sat with my head on my hand, conjuring up memories of my friends of years ago, seeking some clue

173

to her identity, but I could not pierce the veil of mystery surrounding her and at last I went to bed, hoping that perhaps she would reveal herself in my dreams.

A knock on my door woke me at five o'clock. I lit my candle and dressed, then called the innkeeper, whose voice I could hear outside, asking him to convey a message to my benefactor, the Paymaster. I was resolved to see the man who owned this room, this book, this portrait; if necessary, to question him, even at the risk of seeming indiscreet. But I was informed that the officer had gone on duty at four, leaving a message regretting that his early start would deprive him of the pleasure of seeing me. Obviously, the man had deliberately avoided me. There was nothing I could do but try to forget the incident, yet one cannot forget at will.

After breakfast we drove away from Smindoux, and two or three miles further on, when we all dismounted to walk up a hill, our driver made an opportunity to speak to me privately. "Monsieur," he asked, "would you like to know the name of the officer who lent you his room?"

"Of course I would! Haven't I been trying to find out ever since last night? If you know, why in Heaven's name didn't you tell me?"

"He made me promise not to tell you till we were miles away from the camp. He is Monsieur Collard."

"Collard! It was Collard," I repeated, feeling as if a bandage had fallen from my eyes. How often we played together in the woods near home when we were boys! And now he was an exile from France in this lonely Algerian camp! He must have remembered those early days and our old friendship when he offered me his room, but why had he not come to see me, as I would have rushed to meet him again? Suddenly I realized that the woman in the portrait, the prisoner whose face I vaguely recalled, was Marie Cappelle, whom Collard and I had both known as a girl, long before she became notorious as Madame Lafarge.[1] He still cherished her picture;

1. Mme Lafarge, *nee* Marie Cappelle, daughter of Colonel Cappelle and a niece of the secretary general of the Banque de France, first

174

possibly even believed her innocent; and was too proud, too reserved, to greet an old comrade in case I might think less of him for having been a friend, indeed, as I now recalled, a relative, of that unhappy woman. So, poor fellow, he had robbed himself and me of a warm handclasp that would have taken both of us back thirty years. Oh, Collard! How little you knew my heart! How deeply I was wounded by your lack of confidence! "What is the matter?" my friends anxiously inquired when they saw my face, and tears stood in my eyes as I told them.

About two in the afternoon we reached El-Arouch, where, to my great surprise, a deputation was waiting to welcome me in the name of the Third African Regiment, known as the "Zephyrs." Learning of my visit, and wishing to honor me as a playwright, they had arranged a performance of *La Fille de Dominique* and *Farinelli* which they hoped I would enjoy. Since they had heard that I wished to be in Philippeville by nightfall, the entertainment was planned for that very afternoon; the actors were ready and waiting, and the play would begin as soon as I arrived.

Such an invitation, such consideration, moved me more than I can say, and a few moments later I was in their playhouse, where their commanding officer, Captain Plombin, introduced me to the *artistes*, all of them noncommissioned officers and men of the Zephyrs. The actors were remarkably good, all of them true Parisians, to judge from their skill and intelligence, their keen sense of drama and of fun. The hero would have graced any stage in Paris; the comedian kept us in fits of laughter and the singers were in excellent voice. These soldiers

---

came before the French courts when she was convicted of stealing jewels from a fellow guest in the home of the Marquise Marie de Nicolai; in 1840 she was sentenced to life imprisonment for murdering her husband with arsenic, and was a convict at Montpellier at the time Dumas visited Smindoux. She was a woman of great personal charm, and many Frenchmen maintained that she was wrongly convicted. Her mother's uncle, M. Collard, doubtless a relative of Dumas' friend, was one of several influential men who petitioned King and Parliament on her behalf, and she was released a few months before her death in 1852.—*Ed.*

had done everything themselves—built their theater, produced the plays, designed and painted the scenery, arranged all the effects, created the costumes out of anything they found to hand. Our best *couturiers* could not have bettered the dresses worn by the heroine! What if the material was painted canvas and the lace cut out of paper! No one in the audience could have guessed!

Who are these "Zephyrs"? Let me tell you, Madame. In 1831 an order from the War Ministry created three extra battalions to be composed of men under detention for some cause not involving military dishonor, and gave them the special duty of guarding advance posts. The first of these battalions chose the nickname of the "Jackals"; the second, the "Goldfinches"; and the third, the "Zephyrs"; but only the third became well known. Being always stationed at outposts and involved in hazardous enterprises, the Zephyrs had plenty of opportunities of distinguishing themselves, and never missed one. They first won renown at La Makta, in 1833; they were foremost in the first and the second attacks on Constantine; and successfully defended the camp at Djemilah. It was the Zephyrs who held firm at Mazagran, 125 of them routing 6,000 Arabs, a victory so fantastic that the English refused to believe it! "Oh, well!" said their Captain le Lièvre, hearing this, "We'd better do it again!"

In 1836 an official order announced that any Zephyr who distinguished himself by some daring feat, or had for a specified time avoided committing any breach of military discipline, would be promoted to the regular French army, but in offering this encouragement the authorities quite overlooked the fact that the Zephyrs loved their present free and easy life and had no wish to change. So if a Zephyr felt he was in danger of promotion or of being sent away from his beloved Africa to France, he would damage a gun, or steal a pair of shoes, or desert for a day or two—anything to ensure him a few days in the guardhouse.

One Zephyr, detained in a pleasant little guardhouse beside a road, fell into conversation with a passer-by, convinced him

176

that some friends had locked the soldier in as a joke, persuaded him to fetch a locksmith to release him, and, on hearing that the stranger wished to settle in the neighborhood, sold him the house for 1,000 francs down and the balance of the agreed price to be paid over the next five years! Both men signed the bill of sale in the presence of the local man of law, the *sous-seing*, the buyer received a receipt for his 1,000 francs, and the new owner was already installed when the commanding officer came back to camp after the day's maneuvers. The Civil Court at Bougie decided that the contract was valid and refused to take action against the author of such an admirable bit of farce; the military authorities decided to let the matter drop; and the Zephyr returned to camp through a whole series of *arcs de triomphe* erected by his exultant comrades!

Many an archeologist, seeking Roman remains in North Africa, has bought "genuine relics" from a Zephyr, and found later that, though the stone might be ancient, the Latin inscription upon it was the work of a more modern craftsman! The Zephyrs are born naturalists, with the patience and skill to make pets of lizards, snakes, jerboas and other small creatures, occasionally experimenting to produce new species! It was a Zephyr who created the celebrated *"rat-à-trompe"* which so astonished a group of scientists sent from France to study the fauna of Bona! A certain official of the neighborhood, who owned a garden with two fine fig trees, thought it would be interesting to keep chameleons there as pets, and promised a Zephyr a certain price for all he could find. Every day for weeks the Zephyr brought in three or four of these evasive little creatures, until the official had purchased fifty or sixty. Yet, when he looked for them in his garden, he could never find more than a dozen or so. "That is hardly surprising," said the Zephyr airily. "They take the color of the ground, the stones, the leaves of your fig trees, and so cannot be readily seen." The official, not entirely convinced, decided to keep a careful watch, and during the night he saw the Zephyr climb into his garden and collect three or four chameleons from the fig tree, ready to sell them back to their owner

177

the next day. I am still chuckling at a dozen other tales they told me of the tricks they had played on their enemies in the field or the tavern-keepers in villages near their camp.

It was almost five o'clock when we finally said good-by to our new friends, the Zephyrs, who escorted us to the very boundary of El-Arouch. We reached Philippeville at ten, going on early next morning to Stora, where we arrived at eight to find the *Véloce* still riding at anchor waiting for better weather. During my absence a present had arrived for me at Stora—a vulture![2] It was such a ferocious creature that no one would take it on board for me, so I borrowed Desbarolles' horsewhip, took the end of my new pet's chain in my other hand and prepared to drive it along like a turkey cock. It tried very hard to resist, but the whip proved quite effective and soon my vulture was hopping obediently along the road to the jetty, arriving there properly broken in!

All the crew stood waiting on deck to welcome us—for them it was always a special occasion when we came back on board—and in the foremost rank shone the faces of my two sculptors, Hadj'-Younis and his son Ahmed. When I left them, these poor fellows had been terribly afraid that they might not see me again, in which case Heaven knows what would have happened to them! At nine o'clock the *Véloce* set sail and we ran along the coast toward Cape Bugarun in a howling gale, the strong west wind full in our faces, but it proved impossible to round that headland and we were at last forced to take refuge in the anchorage at Collo. This was enemy country, so we could not go ashore to explore the country. Indeed, a couple of gunshots away we could make out a troop of Kabyles[3] fully armed, evidently suspicious of a French warship anchored so close in, and ready to repulse any attempt to land.

At daybreak on the 24th we weighed anchor and set off

2. This vulture, which Dumas named Jugurtha, later formed part of his celebrated menagerie at his Château Monte-Cristo.—*Ed.*

3. The leader of the Kabyles, Abd-el-Kader, did not surrender to the French until December 23, 1847, a year after Dumas' visit to Algeria.—*Ed.*

again. The sea was still very rough, but the wind had dropped, and we made steady progress all that day and the following morning, passing Bougie, Cape Bengut, Cape Matifu, arriving in sight of Algiers at 2 P.M. on December 25. The weather was still extremely unsettled, with sudden violent squalls of wind and rain, though now and then the sun broke through the clouds. All at once, as we watched, a terrific whirlwind swept a cloud of sand from the mountain behind the harbor, threw it over the town like a coffee-colored veil, and even flung it sharply in our faces, though we were well out to sea. A ship running into port ahead of us had to reef all sails and fly before the gale, but we were somewhat sheltered and the power of our engine kept us on our course. A cry of distress drew our eyes to a man in a tiny boat ricocheting from wave to wave like a flat stone bouncing across a pond. We threw him a rope as he passed us but it missed him, and we helplessly watched him swept out to sea, waving his arms in terror. Then a sturdy boat with a pilot and four strong oarsmen shot out in pursuit, and when we berthed beside the jetty a quarter of an hour later we saw the pilot's boat coming back, towing the little craft and the man whose life had been saved at the last moment.

So we reached Algiers at last, and landed just after night-fall on Christmas Day, 1846.

19

ALGIERS REVISITED

We had an important matter to settle as soon as we reached Algiers, the question of the *Véloce*. As you will recall, Madame, when I first arrived there on November 29, Marshal Bugeaud was away. Not knowing precisely when to expect me, he had gone on a visit to the interior, and to avoid wasting my time waiting for his return I took it upon myself to arrange that the *Véloce* should take me on to Tunis. I had persisted in carrying out this plan in spite of scandalized opposition from high administrative circles in Algiers, threatening that if the ship were not placed at my disposal I would immediately return to France and complain to M. de Salvandy, who had sent me on this mission. I could the more readily bare my teeth at all those officious clerks because the credit of 10,000 francs allowed me by the Minister for this tour was still intact, since I had paid for my journey through Spain myself. True, if I returned to Paris I should miss the opportunity of seeing Algeria at government expense, but I should come back at my own and publish an account of everything I saw. So at last they let me have my way, and, as you know, I went to Tunis.[1] Marshal Bugeaud's first task on his return, therefore, was to decide the rights of the case between me and whatever naval officials I had clashed with.

1. Here Dumas gives a much more informative account of how the arrangement was contrived than he did when introducing the subject in ch. 9.—*Ed.*

As soon as I went ashore I inquired whether M. Bugeaud was back in town, and, as it happened, the man I spoke to pointed out the *Maréchal* passing through the street at that moment. In a crisis like this it is my habit to take the bull by the horns, so I went straight up to M. Bugeaud, whom I had met some ten years earlier at the house of M. le comte d'Argout.[2] He recognized me at once, exclaiming: "Ha! So it's you, monsieur! The man who helps himself to a warship when he feels inclined! You don't stint yourself, either! Two hundred and twenty horsepower for your little tour!"

"Monsieur," I replied, quite unruffled, "I have checked the expense sheets with the Captain, and since leaving Cadiz I have cost the government 11,000 francs in food and fuel. Walter Scott, when he visited Italy, cost the English admiralty 130,000 francs, so the French government still owes me 119,000!"

"The devil! In that case, why didn't you tour the whole Mediterranean while you were about it?"

"Simply because I was foolish enough to promise to be back in seventeen days. Actually the trip took nineteen days, but that was no fault of mine. We were delayed by bad weather."

"Oh, well! Now it's over, let's forget about it." He shook me warmly by the hand, adding: "Come and have dinner with me tomorrow. Bring your son and your friends too. Come early, for I shall be holding an investiture of a sheikh, a most interesting man, all-powerful in his own tribe. He is a pure-blooded Kabyle who once served the Duke of Orléans as a guide."

"Ah! El Mokrani, I take it?"

"What? You know him by name? Do Frenchmen at home bother to follow what is going on in Algeria?" The Marshal was so gratified that he chatted away in the friendliest fashion for half an hour, introducing me to General de Bar, who came across the street to join us. At last I managed to drag myself away from these two veterans of the Algerian campaign

2. The Count of Argout (1782–1858) was one of Louis-Philippe's Ministers of State.—*Ed.*

and hurried off to find my friends whom I had left standing in the Rue de la Marine. They had used their time in arranging accommodation for us all at the Hotel de Paris, which had opened only a week before. (Giraud maintains that it always pays to patronize new establishments that have their reputation to make. He assures us that Italians prefer to pray to new saints for the same reason.)

I was in the midst of dressing when my door opened to admit a soldierly figure in civilian dress who came up to me, stood with his feet astride and his hand on my shoulder, and said: "*Parbleu!* So here you are at last, my dear old friend! For ten years I've been hoping to see you again, and this morning, when I saw the *Véloce* in port, I said to myself: 'Good! This time I shall catch him!' What? Don't you recognize me?" Trying my utmost to recall where I had met him, I was murmuring a few commonplaces when he went on: "All right, then, you don't! Never mind! It's not surprising! Since our last meeting I've been made a general. I'm married, too! You still don't know me? I am Yusuf!"

I gave a cry of joy. Here was a friend I had often longed to see once more, yet when I did I failed to recognize him! Not because he was now a general, not because he was married, but because, instead of the romantic Arab-French robes he used to wear, he came to me in a conventional suit that made him look almost as hideous as the rest of us! Naturally we devoted the rest of the day to Yusuf. His carriage was waiting at the door, we all climbed in, and the coachman drove us to Mustapha Supérieur where he has a delightful Arab-style house. His wife, a *Parisienne* with excellent taste, has furnished it entirely in the Arab manner. We were entranced by it and by its wonderful view over the Gulf of Algiers, with part of the town to the left and the plain of Metija to the right.

General Yusuf, the terror of his enemies, hunter of men as well as lions, has one of the sweetest natures I have ever known, and is such a charming host that his guests feel completely at home. We were promised a gigantic *coucousou*[3] for dinner, and to stimulate our appetites we set out to explore the country around Algiers; Giraud, Desbarolles, Alexandre and Maquet on horseback; Yusuf, Boulanger and I in the carriage with Mme Yusuf. As in the suburbs of all Arab towns, the most picturesque sights were the roadside cafés thronged with pilgrims, horses, donkeys and camels; or the fountains where men lay peacefully smoking in the shelter of palms or sycamores, the finest trees in creation and the perfect complement to the African scene.

When we returned, two hours later, we did full justice to a delicious meal served in the courtyard. After dinner Mme Yusuf invited us to walk in her garden, whence had come all the flowers and fruit we had enjoyed at table, and to visit her menagerie, which consisted of an antelope, two gazelles and two ostriches. The antelope seemed to me quite grotesque, with his lyre-shaped horns, his great astonished eyes and his enormous head; the gazelles, with their slender legs, restless ears, quick, bright eyes, had all the charm that Arab poets praise, but, beyond all doubt, the ostriches were the most fantastic creatures I had ever seen. Our hostess had suggested we should take them some bread, and each of us was carrying enough to satisfy a starving man, but our store vanished in the twinkling of an eye without dulling the edge of their appetites. They swallowed Mme Yusuf's gloves and our own as well, each mouthful forming a lump that took a whole minute to travel visibly down their long necks. One bird even filched a gold pin, two or three inches long, from Madame's hair, and swallowed it without hesitation. The only thing that caused them the slightest difficulty was Alexandre's handkerchief which he tied into a dozen knots before offering one end to each bird. Their beaks met in the middle, they wrestled for a few moments and seemed about to fight, then the male gallantly gave way as gentlemen do, and we watched the

3. A typical North African dish of millet flour, meat and leaves of the baobab tree, steamed with a kind of broth.—*Ed.*

knots move steadily down the female's throat like a string of trucks on a railway. Desbarolles, anxious not to lose his opera hat, was careful to keep at a safe distance from these omnivorous creatures, and we did not blame him. When, after a thoroughly enjoyable day, we at last returned to our hotel we talked of Mme Yusuf's ostriches half the night.

Algiers, headquarters of the dreaded Barbary pirates ever since the Middle Ages, the traditional stronghold of the Deys who defied Europe for centuries, suffered considerable damage during the bombardment that preceded the victory of our forces in 1830. Except for the Grand Mosque, which survived, all the lower part of the town behind the harbor was demolished, and has now been rebuilt in the French manner. However, parts of the ancient city of the Deys still stand on the steep hill beyond, where the Bab-el-Oued, the "River Gate," leads to a street that climbs five hundred steps to the Casbah, the old palace and citadel, from which the Dey fled through one door as French troops entered by another.

We spent our second afternoon and evening exploring these preserves of the Prophet. In the sixteenth century a Moslem seer foretold: "Woe to thee, Algiers, for the Franks shall tread in mastery through thy streets, and thy sons' daughters shall open their doors to them." Never has a prophecy been more accurately fulfilled. With our Arab-speaking guides we knocked at certain doors in the old town that readily opened to offer us a welcome that was certainly cordial, if not entirely disinterested. Such houses were much the same as others of that type we had visited in Tunis, the only difference being that there the girls were invariably Jewesses, while here they were all Moorish and rather more sophisticated, for their robes were embroidered in gold and silver (except where they were transparent), and they could speak a few words of French. (Such words! Good God! Soldiers and sailors are terrible language teachers!) I might add that they were completely shameless, without the least pretense of modesty.

Most of these unfortunate girls were not even born when

the French captured Algiers. What drove them into prostitution? Sheer grinding poverty! Why were they all of Moorish blood? How had it come about that the Moors, who were so wealthy while the Turks ruled the country, had sunk to such poverty under French domination? Our guides were surprised at my questions, which, apparently, no one had thought to ask before, but after some reflection they gave me this reply. In the old days the Moors were the richest men in Algiers, owning houses which they let at high rents, cattle that they bred and sold, land that produced good crops for market. When the French came, they, like many other native civilians, were terrified and chose to flee into the interior, first selling, not their houses and lands, for these no one would buy, but their household possessions and their jewels, at a fraction of their true value. On the proceeds they lived for two or three years of voluntary exile, then, learning that no harm had come to the citizens of Algiers, they drifted back and once more took possession of their houses and lands. Gradually confidence grew, the price of houses doubled, even quadrupled, between 1830 and 1835, and the exiles who returned early made immense fortunes at that period. But those who had fled furthest—to Smyrna, Cairo, Constantinople—and in general these were the Moors, were the last to return, and found on arrival that the French civilians then coming to settle in Algiers wished to rent, not buy, houses.

The Moors were not unduly perturbed, for they firmly believed that very soon the Prophet would answer their prayers and drive the French from Algeria. Meanwhile, for a lump sum paid in advance, they leased their property to French immigrants at a nominal rent, overlooking the fact that the tenants, wise in European custom, had reserved the right to renew the lease indefinitely at the same rent. But the Prophet was in no hurry to grant his worshipers' petition; the French continued to rule Algiers, and the Moors were ruined. They had nothing left to sell but their daughters, and so the ancient prophecy was fulfilled. But though Moorish girls entertain Frenchmen in this fashion, make no mistake, they still hate them, for the bitter enmity between their race and ours can never be overcome. It is fostered by too many contrasts.

Their religion promises a sensual paradise, ours a spiritual. A Frenchman can marry one wife only, and adultery is punishable by law; a Moslem may have four wives and all the concubines he can afford to support. French women walk freely in the streets, their faces uncovered; Arab women are prisoners in their homes, and if they venture out they must be heavily veiled. If an Arab's household is quarrelsome, he restores peace with a good strong stick; a Frenchman who strikes a woman is dishonored. The more wives an Arab has, the richer he is; one wife is often enough to make a Frenchman bankrupt. An Arab marries as soon as he can; a Frenchman as late in life as possible. We are almost always troubled and careworn; an Arab, never, for, to him, whatever happens is the will of Allah.

We travel for pleasure; an Arab only when he must. We wear tight clothes, like to keep our feet warm and our heads cool. They choose loose, flowing robes, swathe their heads in a turban and leave their feet bare. With us, painting is an art; with them, a sin. We lock up a madman; they hold him sacred. A Frenchman's honor forbids him to yield a single step in a battle or a duel; an Arab may flee without disgrace. We are gay, they are grave; we drink wine with our meals; wine is forbidden to them, and they drink only when they have finished eating. We treat our parents familiarly, with more affection than respect; but an Arab would not sit, smoke or speak without permission in the presence of his father, or, indeed, of his elder brother. When our faith decrees a day of fasting, it causes us no hardship; with them, from the moment the morning light is strong enough for him to tell a white thread from a black one, an Arab is forbidden to eat, drink, smoke or embrace his wife till night has fully come. To us, their swift revenge seems merciless; to them, our law's delays, our legal casuistries, are the very negation of justice.

The French interpretation of justice is at the root of many bitter misunderstandings between the Arabs and ourselves.

186

Here is an example of what can happen. There may be two adjacent plots of land, one belonging to an Arab, the other sold to a Frenchman. The Arab is not worried, for the boundary between them is clearly established, a matter of common knowledge, but soon the European begins to build a house, not on his own plot but on his neighbor's land. The Arab would be only too glad to take the matter into his own hands, but the law forbids him, so he goes to find the *chef-du-bureau* of his village or neighborhood and presents his case. This official goes to see the truth of the matter with his own eyes, then opens proceedings with a polite letter to the Frenchman, pointing out that he has made a mistake. The intruder receives the letter, but has no need to be polite and does not reply.

The Arab, seeing that all this has had no effect and that his neighbor is still laying more bricks, goes back to the *chef-du-bureau*, who tells him there is nothing more he can do. The Arab must apply to the *juge de paix*. In due course, the *juge* summons the plaintiff and the defendant to appear before him, but the Frenchman does not attend, so after hearing the facts the *juge* sends him an order to quit, and the Arab goes home to tell the assembled villagers that the French authorities have dealt justly with him. Never dreaming that anyone would dare to disobey an order made by a judge, he waits for his neighbor to go away, but the Frenchman stays, and the house rises higher and higher. The Arab waits a little longer, believing in his simplicity that some severe penalty must shortly fall on the trespasser, but at last he goes back to the *chef-du-bureau*, who explains that he must now take his case to the magistrate's court, and tells him that, above all, he must have a good solicitor.

The Arab, who is learning several new words, finds out what a solicitor is, goes to see one, and tells him his story. The man of law comments that it is an excellent case and sure to succeed, but first the Arab must pay him 25 francs. The Arab replies that he will call again, and goes back to ask the *chef-du-bureau* why he must pay 25 francs to a man he does not know, in order to stop another stranger stealing his field.

187

"It is the custom," replies the *chef*, so the Arab goes sadly to dig up the stone under which he has buried his little store of money, takes out 5 duros, and counts them out to the solicitor one by one, with a heavy sigh for each. When the case against the European comes to court, let us suppose the interpreter is a good one, the chief magistrate is able to grasp the situation, and a verdict is given for the plaintiff.

Again he goes home and waits, watching the roof being put on the new house, and sixteen days later a paper is put into his hand, which he takes to the *chef-du-bureau*. It is written from left to right, not from right to left in the Arab manner, and the letters are small, not large, but at last it is deciphered and found to be a notice that the Frenchman has appealed against the verdict. Now the case must be heard in Algiers, at great expense; later, perhaps, in Paris, where costs will be still higher. But our poor Arab has spent all his money; he has not been able to plant a crop on his field and has lost his harvest, so he calls his friends together, declares bitterly that all the Christians, and in particular the French government, have conspired to swindle him out of everything he had. He flees into the desert, and soon the Frenchman can claim that he has been in possession of the house for three years and is therefore the legal owner of the property, including the land.

In the old days, the Arab would have made his complaint before the Cadi on a market day, the Cadi would have consulted the old men of the village, they would have confirmed where the true boundary lay, the field would have been restored to its rightful owner, and the swindler would have received fifty blows on the soles of his feet. Fresh proof that the merchant who sold cotton nightcaps in Tunis was wrong to prefer French justice to Turkish justice!

20

FAREWELL TO AFRICA

Next morning we received word from Marshal Bugeaud that the investiture of El Mokrani had been postponed to January 1, so we decided to devote the last two days of the old year to visiting Blida. We managed to find seats in an omnibus of sorts and were soon en route for that lovely little town of orange groves.

On the main road, a short distance beyond Bufarik, we saw a pillar with the inscription: "To the memory of twenty-two brave men who died in action at Beni-Mered on April 10, 1842," with no indication as to who they were. I learned that the contractor who prepared this monument found that the cost exceeded the funds available, so he economized by omitting the names of the men who fell. Here is their story. On that day a squad of eighteen soldiers led by Sergeant Blaudan, accompanied by a doctor, a brigadier and a guide, were carrying mail from Bufarik to Mered when they were attacked by a force of Arabs on a bridge over a ravine. There was at Beni-Mered a blockhouse equipped with two or three semaphores, and these were hastily manipulated to send word to Bufarik. Thirty men, soldiers and civilians in the streets of the town, instantly leapt on the first horses they could find and galloped out to bring help. They drove the Arabs back, but were too late to save Sergeant Blaudan, whom they found mortally wounded but still trying to rally his dead or dying men. "It was time you came," he breathed as he collapsed in their arms. Back in Bufarik, he raved in delirium, yelling: "Keep firing!" but at the last he had a moment of calm. Colonel Morris, watching at his bedside, placed his own cross in the sergeant's hands, Blaudan raised it to his lips, and so died.

Two hours later we were at Blida. Looking at this town today, with its big square houses, their wide windows recklessly admitting the all-devouring African sunshine, it is difficult to imagine what it used to be like when it contained only rows of Arab huts, almost lost behind its orchards of orange trees and its thick cactus hedges. Yet no modern changes can rob it of its wonderful setting on the lowest slopes of the Atlas Mountains, its view over the fertile plains of the Metija, watered by the broad river Wad-el-Keber, or its bitter-sweet savor of bygone glories, and if Blida is no longer quite the marvel it used to be, it is still a lovely jewel.

We were given a cordial welcome by the commander of the battalion stationed there, whose name was Bourbaki. He struck me as a perfect example of what a French officer should be, elegant, handsome, daring, and it did not surprise me that even here in Algeria, where all our men are brave, Bourbaki's courage has become proverbial. Like most soldiers who have spent long years in Africa, Bourbaki has developed a sincere respect and admiration for the Arabs and a supreme contempt for all those speculators and adventurers who have descended on the country like a plague. Indeed, the general opinion about such commercial tricksters is aptly conveyed by an Arab proverb: "All the honest men who have come to Algeria from France came by land."

Bourbaki, talking of Arab justice, gave us an illuminating story of certain incidents that recently took place in the very spot where we stood. A man came before the tribunal of Jaya, the Aga of Blida, and confessed that, finding his wife in adultery with his neighbor, he had shot the man dead.

"What happened to your wife?" asked the Aga.

"I love her so much that I forgave her and let her live."

"Lead this man away to execution," Jaya ordered his guards. "He is a murderer."

A week later another Arab, in his hand a dagger still dripping with blood, came to the Aga as he sat in the market place to pronounce judgments.

"What have you done?" asked Jaya. "Whose blood is this?"

"The blood of my wife and her lover. I caught them together and killed them."

"Both of them?" Jaya inquired.

"Both!"

"That is well. Take these 500 francs to buy yourself another wife, and go in peace."

When the Aga was asked to explain his different treatment of these two men, both guilty of murder, he replied: "The first, who chose to kill only one of the guilty pair, was an assassin. The second, who killed both, performed an act of justice."

Bourbaki had arranged for us an excursion into the mountains, where we were invited to dine with the *marabout* of Sidi-Capschi and his friends. These men, who were to be our hosts, were the hereditary owners of these plains before the war. We seized their lands, drove them into the mountains, and in exchange offered them an alliance with France. A great honor for them, no doubt, but to men who considered themselves the natural lords of the country it may well have seemed rather inadequate. Yet Bourbaki told us of many Arabs who have respected that alliance and served our cause with a strange, almost fanatical loyalty. In particular I remember his praise for Ahmet-ben-Kadour, formerly sheikh of the Guerrouans and now Cadi of the Beni-Khetils, who served General Changarnier[1] as a guide during the Metija campaign against the Kabyles. Their leader, Abd-el-Kader, threatened to slaughter his wife and children unless he agreed to desert or betray the General, but Ahmet refused. "Tell Abd-el-Kader," he replied proudly, "that I am rich enough to buy another wife and young enough to father other children. His threats will not move me to break the promise I have given."

1. General N. A. T. Changarnier became Governor of Algeria in April 1848.—*Ed.*

Bourbaki spoke, too, of that great virtue for which our enemies are famous—Arab hospitality. A traveler arrives at a *douair*, literally a ring of tents, taking care to strike his spurs noisily against his stirrups to warn the women to keep out of sight. When the owner of a tent hears this signal and comes out, the stranger approaches him, saying: *"Dif-Erbi*— a guest sent by Allah." *"Marhaba-bik,"* is the reply, meaning: "Such a guest is welcome." The host assists him to dismount, takes him into the tent, spreads a rug for him to lie upon, and makes sure his horse is well cared for. Whether the stranger is rich or poor, he need have no fear for his weapons or his other possessions. Everything will be safe and will be handed to him intact when he leaves. A meal is set before him, and the host calls in his neighbors to help entertain the guest, but at the first sign of weariness they all depart, leaving the stranger to sleep in peace. If when morning comes he wishes to stay longer, he will still be welcome, but if he must go his horse will be saddled and waiting for him. He mounts and says: *"Erbi ikelef alikoun*—may God requite you," and rides away. No one has inquired his name or where he is going, and his host is fully recompensed by a word of thanks.

Colonel Daumas, who collaborated with Ausone de Chancel to write those two magnificent works, *Sahara* and *Caravan*, told me this story: "One day, I and a friend of mine sought shelter in this way in Glea, a little village to the west of Beni-Mezab. Our host had a little son, a lovely child of eight or ten, and we spent part of the day playing with him, but toward evening he ran off and we did not see him again. When the father brought our supper we inquired after the boy, but paid no attention to the sadness that showed for a moment in our host's face, or a certain note in his voice as he replied: "He is asleep." In the morning, as we were preparing to leave, the father came to us and said: "My honored guests, last night you inquired for my son. He was playing with his friends, jumping from one rooftop to the next, when he fell and was killed. I replied as I did because you were so kind to the boy, and I feared that the truth would spoil your supper and disturb your night's rest. Allah will forgive the lie because my intention was good. You enjoyed your meal and slept well, unaware that Death was your fellow guest in my home. Now I go to follow the body of my only child to the place of burial. Will you come with me?"

The story moved me deeply, and I stayed awhile in the hotel at Blida to record it in the General's own words, also to complete my notes on the day's events, while Bourbaki and some other officers rode out to Sidi-Capschi with Giraud, Alexandre, Boulanger, Maquet, Ausone de Chancel and Desbarolles. About four o'clock a messenger came to warn me that it was time for me to be on my way if I was to spend an hour or two with our host, Mohammed, so I jumped astride the horse he had brought for me and we trotted briskly through the streets of Blida, quickening our pace to a gallop as we left the town. A jackal crossed our path and I could not resist chasing it over the open plain, but dusk was falling and we soon lost sight of it in the long grass. My companion was careful to ride close beside me because the route we had to follow was treacherous and thickly crowded with storage pits which are hard enough to distinguish by daylight, and at night are very dangerous.

About half-past six we reached an Arab village on one of the first ridges of the Atlas, where we were anxiously awaited, not only by our hosts but even more by our fellow guests, who were half dead with hunger. We all met in the House of Strangers, a large building in the market place, open on all four sides to show that visitors were welcome from every direction. One curious thing, showing that the house was intended for European as well as Arab guests, was the fact that it was furnished with tables and chairs, in addition to the customary profusion of mats, cushions and carpets. We were offered milk, sweet or curdled, chickens and ducks swimming in gravy, and an immense *coucousou*. As an indication of the degree of civilization our hosts had acquired, I will add that we were provided with spoons and forks at table, and Mohammed offered me a pinch of snuff from a tin that had formerly contained a paste made by a well-known manufacturing chemist of Paris.

We spent the evening smoking, drinking coffee and enjoying the company of our new friends, until at eleven o'clock Bourbaki warned us it was time to leave, and with warm-hearted regrets we said farewell. We set out for Blida through driving rain, the night so dark that we could not even see the heads of our horses, still less could we guide them down the steep slopes we had to negotiate. Bourbaki advised us to let the reins lie loose on their necks and trust to their instinct, and in this way we came safely down to more level ground. The rain grew heavier and heavier, as though the very clouds of Algeria had combined to wish me good-by, and to make things worse the road was so bad that we had to slacken our speed to walking pace. In half an hour we were just so many filters, the water pouring in at the necks of our shirts and out again at our boots.

Our conversation, brisk at first, grew spasmodic and finally ceased altogether as we pressed forward in Indian file beside a track that was far more like a river than a road. Somewhere a clock began to strike slowly, and we counted the notes of its bronze hammer. Twelve. We had just crossed that invisible dividing line between one year and the next; 1846 had passed us safely into 1847, and had itself slipped away to join eternity. I thought of all my friends, one by one. How surprised they would be if they could have known I was sending them good wishes for the New Year from the plains of Metija, shivering with cold, drenched from head to foot, riding slowly along through torrential rain such as we have no idea of in France!

Ten minutes later we were in Bufarik, where, thanks to Bourbaki, a warm room and a good meal awaited us. Next morning, as we climbed into the omnibus for Algiers, we felt once more the sadness of parting from friends we had known only for a day but with whom it would be sweet to spend a lifetime, well aware that in all probability we should never meet again.

*   *   *

We were greatly looking forward to attending the reception in Algiers to honor El Mokrani, for he was a very important personage among the Arabs, and, by arranging that it should take place on New Year's Day, Marshal Bugeaud had invested the occasion with a special solemnity. We duly presented ourselves at one o'clock and found the ceremony about to begin. The hall was crowded with muftis, cadis and their assistants, all authorities on Mohammedan law; *oukils,* the leaders of various religious sects; *ulémas,* versed in the laws of native tribes; loyal chiefs from the territories round Algiers, with their retinues; and finally the hero of the day, the new Caliph of the Medjana, Seid-Achmet-ben-Mohammed-El Mokrani, accompanied by his young son and other members of his family.

The ceremony began with the customary kissing of hands. By a fortunate chance, the Mohammedan year had ended almost at the same time as our own,[2] and the Marshal had the additional pleasure of being able to respond to his guests' new year greetings with similar good wishes to them. Then the chief mufti, a venerable man of eighty, spoke on behalf of the peoples of Algeria, assuring the Marshal of their good will and their prayers that God would make France even more happy and prosperous, if that were possible.

Then the Marshal addressed the gathering with his customary vivid clarity and happy turns of phrase, explaining to the Arabs that Algeria's welfare depended on three important matters that demanded all their attention: Peace, Justice and

2. The Mohammedan calendar is dated from the flight of Mahomet from Mecca to Medina (by our reckoning, July 15, 622). Each year consists of twelve lunar months, and New Year's Day thus falls earlier in the season every year, completing the cycle in about 32½ years. At the time of Dumas' visit, the Mohammedan New Year's Day corresponded with Sunday, December 20, 1846.—*Ed.*

195

Agriculture. "Peace is my responsibility," he continued. "I have promised you to maintain peace, and I will keep my word." El Mokrani made a sign that he wished to comment. *"Monsieur le maréchal,"* he said, "we are all fully persuaded that your government cannot be other than peaceful, for good men cannot fail to appreciate the benefits you bring, and an evil man knows he cannot escape your wrath."

"Justice," the Marshal went on, "is administered by those of your own people whom you yourselves have chosen to fulfill the high office of judges. They act under our supervision and direction. If any man has occasion to complain, let him come to me, and I will ensure that he receives justice." Then the Chief Cadi, in the name of the Moslem magistrates, thanked the Marshal for the confidence he had placed in native judges, assuring him that they would ever strive to be worthy of the honor, and conscientiously fulfill their important functions.

"Agriculture," M. Bugeaud continued, "is the fruit of peace. War is a threefold scourge, for poverty and famine follow in its wake. Therefore again I promise you peace, and this, with God's help in preserving you from droughts and locusts, is to promise you a time of plenty."

Then he signaled to El Mokrani to come forward, and ceremoniously presented him with a musket, saying: "Use this against lions and the enemies of France." On the new Caliph's shoulders he placed a burnoose of red cloth decorated with gold lace, and bestowed on him a length of silk from Lyons as a gift to his wives. El Mokrani's own gun was standing beside the seat he had occupied, a magnificent weapon all damascened in silver and resplendent with coral, worth at least ten times as much as the musket he had just received from the Marshal. His young son was wearing a robe of such superb quality cashmere that the most elegant *Parisienne* would have coveted it. As for the red and gold burnoose vouchsafed to him by the royal munificence of France to honor his investiture, he would scarcely have deemed it fit for his lackey to wear. Beyond question, his tents held rolls of those

196

superb tissues woven at Fez or embroidered in Tunis, beside which the finest products of Lyons look as coarse as a woollen shawl against a gossamer veil from India. But El Mokrani was a man of the world, and gave every indication of prizing the Marshal's gifts above anything he possessed, bowing low and pouring out his thanks with all the flowery exaggeration so natural to his race.

The investiture thus accomplished, the Marshal turned to the Cadi of the Chenouas, Kassem-ben-Djalloud, and thanked him in the name of France for the assistance he and his tribe had given, a fortnight earlier, to the crew of a vessel shipwrecked on their coast, rescuing them from certain death in the stormy seas. (If the ship had been wrecked on the same rocks two years ago, not a man would have been spared. Every head would have rolled in the sand.) The Cadi gravely replied: "I am overwhelmed, *Monsieur le maréchal,* by the compliments you have deigned to pay me. I simply did what I considered was my duty, as a true Moslem should."

So the ceremony was concluded and all the audience withdrew, except the new Caliph and his son, who were to dine with us. "Now," said the Marshal to us, "you shall see for yourselves how far the French and the Arabs really understand one another." Then, turning to El Mokrani, he went on: "My government has accorded you a grant of 12,000 francs on your appointment as Caliph of Medea."

"I shall place that sum in your hands on the due date, complete to the last farthing," replied El Mokrani, bowing low. As an Arab it had never entered his head that he would receive payment for exercising control over his new subjects. He fully expected to have to pay for the privilege. We took advantage of the opportunity to question him ourselves. "How many sons have you?" I asked. "Three." "And daughters?" He had never bothered to inquire. I asked if he knew anything of the towns known as Carthage, Babylon, or Tyre. He answered: "The cord that holds up an Arab's tent is no more than a cord, yet it has seen the fall of all the towns you speak of."

197

After fifteen minutes we were on the friendliest terms, and he confided to us that he was suffering from a horrible disease that is commoner than one would expect in the interior of the country. What he needed, more than anything else in the world, was to see a good doctor, and Chancel, who had lived in Algiers for three years, promised to take him personally, first thing in the morning, to the finest specialist in the town.

That evening and the next day we were busy with preparations for departure. How quickly those last hours passed! We were still reproaching ourselves for not having done half the things we meant to do in Algiers when we boarded the *Orénoque,* which was to take us back to France, at ten o'clock in the morning of January 3. The *Véloce* was moored a few hundred yards away, crowded with my good friends, who would have been astonished if they could have heard M. Léon de Maleville declaring in the Chamber of Deputies that my presence on board her had dishonored the French flag! (Naturally, having made such a statement, M. de Maleville took refuge in the inviolability of the Tribune, but it is as well that his words should be generally known, and I therefore print them here.)

All the officers of the *Véloce* were on deck, Commandant Bérard at their head; every member of the crew was clinging to the rigging, waving caps and handkerchiefs; and as the *Orénoque* sailed nearer we all exchanged a last loud cry of *Adieu.* For a whole hour after I could see her no more I stood silent and still, thinking over all the good times I had known with these gallant officers, these true-hearted sailormen, who found it just as reasonable to lend a ship to a poet as to a third or fourth attaché of some embassy!

Soon, as we drew away, the ship, the town, the mountains themselves disappeared like a dream. Africa became no more than a cloud on the horizon, then vanished in her turn, though I retained her hostages in the two artists I was bringing from Tunis to carve Arab sculpture for my château of Monte-Cristo. After a very pleasant crossing of only thirty-nine hours we entered the port of Toulon on the evening of January 4. Contrary to what one might expect, my heart always feels a strong emotion when, after a long voyage, I once more set foot in France. Petty enmities, jealousies, long-standing hatreds lie in wait for me there—how glad I should be if it were otherwise!—but I am not unduly cast down, for beyond her frontiers I have heard the verdict of posterity.

Alexandre Dumas' *Adventures in Russia* will soon be published in America for the first time by Chilton Company—Book Division

Index

❦ ❦ ❦

Arab and Moorish women—(*Cont.*)
  dress of, 115
  illiteracy of, 115, 170–171
  imagination of, 115–117
  lack of individuality of, 113
  Moorish dancers, 169–172
  prostitutes in Algiers, 184–186
  sensual pleasures of, 114, 115
  sterility of, curing of, 120, 121–
    122
  veiling of, 117, 122, 186
  vengeance shown by, 118–119
  wives, desire of to please hus-
    bands, 117
    divorcing of, 113
    love affairs of, 117–118
    unfaithful, punishment of, 112,
      117, 169
    unlimited number of, 113, 186
Arab beaters, 33, 36, 37
Arabian Nights, 129
Arabs, adultery among, 117, 186
  customs of, comparison of with
    French customs, 186–188
  destruction of Roman Carthage
    by, 126
  hospitality of, 192–194
  justice of, 190–191
    tribal, 162–167
  outcast, in Tangier, 15
  rescue of French prisoners from,
    61–72, 73–74, 81
  women (*see* Arab and Moorish
    women)
Argout, Count of, 181
Arsenal of Goletta, 86
Atlas Mountains, 81, 190, 193
Augustine, Saint, 146, 147
Austerlitz, battle at, 10, 78
Autran, M., 6
Azencot, David, 25–30, 33, 34, 36,
    41–45, 48–49

Bab-el-Oued, 184
Bab-el-Souika, 109
Bach mameluke, 110, 129, 134, 135
Bagarun, Cape, 178
Ball at French Consulate in Tunis,
    124, 133–136

Ballad on bombardment of Tan-
    gier, 44
Barbary pirates, 184
Barber shop in Tunis, 103–104
Barbut, Sergeant Major, 70
Bardo, 106, 108, 111, 112, 119, 140
Barometers in Gibraltar, uselessness
    of, 57
Bastinado, 37
Bastinga Point, 69
Battue, 36, 39
Baylen, capitulation at, 77
Bayonnaise, La, 130
Bazaars of Tunis, 100–104, 137–138,
    142, 169
Beaters, Arab, 33, 36, 37
Beauty of Arab and Moorish
    women, 114, 170
  loss of with age and child-bear-
    ing, 114
Bedeau, General, 161, 162, 168, 172
Belus, 125–126
Ben-Afroun, 80–81
Bengut, Cape, 179
Beni-Bouillafars, 63–64, 69
Beni-Khetils, 191
Beni-Mered, monument at, 189
Beni-Snanens, 75
  trapping of at Cape Melonia, 73
Bérard, Captain, 2, 4, 5, 16, 62–64,
    68–69, 72, 74, 77, 81, 83, 87,
    95, 148–149, 152, 198
Berbers, 162
Bey, of Oran, 118–119
  of Tetuán, 48, 64, 65
  of Tunis, 86–94, 99
    visit to palace of, 105–109, 139–
      140
Bird hunting in Bizerta, 83–85, 87
Biskris, 162
Bizerta, 82–85
  bird hunting in, 83–85, 87
  fortifications of, 83, 84
  hospitality in, 85
  Turkish cemetery in, 83
  vegetation of, 84
Blaudan, Sergeant, 189, 190
Blida, 189, 190, 193, 194
Boabs, 140